I0202967

LEGACY
Leadership®

The Biblical Standard

for Christian Leaders

CoachWorks®
The **LEGACY** Leader Company

CoachWorks® International
Dallas, Texas USA
www.CoachWorks.com
www.LegacyLeadership.com

ISBN # 978-0-9801965-8-0

LEGACY LEADERSHIP® THE BIBLICAL STANDARD FOR CHRISTIAN LEADERSHIP. Copyright 2005. Revised 2014. CoachWorks® International, Inc., Dallas, Texas USA. All rights reserved. The Legacy Leadership Model, Program and System was written and developed by Dr. Lee Smith and Dr. Jeannine Sandstrom. No part of this publication may be reproduced in any form, or by any means whatsoever without written permission from the publisher, except in the case of brief quotations embodied in critical articles and reviews with appropriate acknowledgements.

CoachWorks®, Legacy Leader®, Legacy Leaders®, Legacy Leadership®, The Legacy Leadership® 5 Best Practices™, The Legacy Leadership 5 Best Practices At-A-Glance™, The Legacy Leadership System™, The Legacy Leadership Model™, LegacyPursuit™, The Legacy Leadership Competency Inventory (LLCI)™, LeaderShifts™, Legacy Leadership Program™, The Legacy Counsel (TLC)™, The Legacy Forum™, Legacy Leader Coach™, Executive Workout™, Collaborative Conversation™, Holder of Vision and Values™, Creator of Collaboration and Innovation™, Influencer of Inspiration and Leadership™, Advocator of Differences and Community™, Calibrator of Responsibility and Accountability™, Inside Out Shifts™, and RealTime Legacy™.

Printed in USA. CoachWorks® Press, Dallas, TX USA. Legacy Leadership® logo, cover design and layout by deskWorks, Woodinville, WA.

If you would like further information about the Legacy Leadership® Program and other CoachWorks® services and products, please contact us at info@CoachWorks.com.

Bible Translations Referenced:

The Holy Bible, New International Version® (NIV), Copyright © 1973, 1978, 1984 Colorado Springs, Colorado: International Bible Society.

The Holy Bible, New King James Version, (NKJV) Copyright © 1982 Nashville, Tennessee: Thomas Nelson, Inc. 1982.

Holy Bible, New Living Translation (NLT). Copyright © 1996, Wheaton, IL: Tyndale House Publishers, Inc.

Holy Bible, The New Century Version (NCV), Copyright © 1987, 1988, 1991, Dallas, Texas: Word Publishing.

The Message: The Bible in Contemporary Language, by Eugene H. Peterson, Copyright © 2002, NAVPress, Colorado Springs, Colorado.

CoachWorks®
The LEGACY Leader Company

COACHWORKS INTERNATIONAL
Dallas, Texas USA
www.CoachWorks.com
www.LegacyLeadership.com

Legacy Leadership®: The Biblical Standard for Christian Leaders. © 2005-2014 COACHWORKS® International. Dallas, TX USA. All Rights Reserved.

Table of Contents

Legacy Leadership®: The Biblical Standard for Christian Leadership

*Legacy Leadership®: **The Biblical Standard for Christian Leaders.*** © 2005-2014 COACHWORKS® International. Dallas, TX USA. All Rights Reserved.

What is Legacy?

How do you define *legacy*? It's a word we hear bouncing and buzzing frequently around bookstores and TV talk shows these days. It was originally thought to imply the fortune, or lack thereof, that one would *leave behind* for his or her heirs. Today it has come to signify what people are known for (their "brand" or reputation), how they are remembered after their passing. Do you know what your legacy will be? Will it be something you are remembered for only when you're gone? What if you were *living* your legacy now? What if your vision for the future, your legacy, is evident in everything you do, every day? It can happen. Legacy Leadership is about *living* your legacy, not just *leaving* it.

It's who we are and what we live today that shapes our legacy for tomorrow.

Living your legacy means making a dedicated investment in the better future of others. This isn't about money, financial investment or material wealth and capital building. Legacy Leadership is not about building things. It is about building people. It is about investing your time, your energy, your competencies and your interest and concern in individuals who then share what they have learned with others, maximizing the return on your investment. While this book is primarily concerned with leadership legacy in business, this simple formula for human investment is applicable to every area of life—family, community, *and* business. Each of us can be a leader in our respective environments. In a basic sense, a leader is one who shows the way, who escorts or guides others. A *Legacy* Leader guides others into a better future—into *being* better, *doing* better, and *leading* better. Your best self is offered to others in order to develop their best selves and so on, leaving a multi-generational imprint—a living legacy.

Legacy Leaders

It seems that Legacy Leaders all have the SAME right stuff.

We can all tell stories or remember details about the lives, careers, and accomplishments of noted leaders today and in history. While there were, and are, many good or excellent leaders among us, only certain "greats" garner a sort of language and emotion that separates them from other leaders, creating lasting influence. If you listen carefully, you will hear it too. The stories are laced with the *language of legacy*—captured in the 5 Practices of Legacy Leadership. We call these men and women Legacy Leaders. And it seems that Legacy Leaders all have the *same* right stuff.

Some of these leaders are known well, and draped in titles, medals, decorations, awards, achievements and accomplishments. These are impressive and noteworthy, but do not make the Legacy Leader. Some are high profile; others remain behind the scenes. Some are businesspeople; others are not. We can tell you stories of dozens of men and women, everyday folks, who have profoundly influenced others and lived lives of true leadership legacy. They don't all share the public eye, and they don't all have an arm's-length list of noted accomplishments. What they *do* all have is the same stuff that makes a leader a *Legacy* Leader. This is what Legacy Leadership is all about—identifying and defining the right stuff of leaders of legacy.

Legacy Leaders are found in every walk of life, from the boardroom to the battlefield, from public service to private homes, neighborhoods, schools and communities. They are found in the worn pages of history books, the memories of those who have been touched by them, and they continue to inspire and influence present and future leaders.

Recognized or relatively unknown, in business or life in general, the world is hungry for these kind of leaders—*Legacy* Leaders. They are leaders who intentionally influence others. Influencing is at the core of their being, and drives the behaviors, skills and competencies of all the practices of Legacy Leadership. It is what allows the leader to live his or her legacy today, and to grow the leaders of tomorrow. In small ways, or grand strokes, these leaders change our world.

Legacy and Influence

Legacy in leadership is not about leaving something behind—it is about influencing others enough to cause change, a shift from unconsciously doing leadership to consciously *being* a leader. The best way to do that is to influence in person, by living legacy today, not waiting for others to reflect on the past tomorrow.

We all influence, whether we know it or not. In fact, we cannot *not* influence. *Whether* we influence is not the question. It's *how* we influence—positively or negatively, intentionally or accidentally. Are we mindful and conscious about influence, or completely unaware of our impact on others? Many think of influencing only as a method to obtain what they want. **We cannot NOT influence.** This is not the kind of influence we're discussing here. They are merely *using* influence to gain power, money, favor, status or whatever it is that satisfies *self*. This is an important distinction. Using influence for self-centered gain is deception. Intentionally influencing for selfless positive relationships and growth is legacy.

Influence is the heart of legacy. Understanding how your personal and professional legacy of influence works is critical to understanding Legacy Leadership, and critical to positively impacting others. A strong, positive person of intentional influence possesses a demeanor, a certain knowing, and an instant and irresistible attraction or connection with others. We are reminded of a tribute we read of the passing of such a leader: *"... someone who quickly and easily earned my respect ... there was an intangible about him in this way unlike anyone I have*

Legacy Leadership®: The Biblical Standard for Christian Leaders. © 2005-2014 COACHWORKS® International. Dallas, TX USA. All Rights Reserved.

ever met." Intentional influence is a characteristic and attitude that draws people. This individual called the leader's influence an "intangible." We would give this intangible a name—*presence.*

There's a lot to be said for the power of presence. You have most likely known people like this—those with whom you desired company, learning and acceptance. And the most peculiar thing about these people is that others seem to want to work hard to please them, to be their best selves, be more like them. There is a saying that captures this quality: *"Our best friends are those in whose presence we can be our best selves."* People who positively influence are those in whose presence we can be our best selves, do our best work, and reach our best potential.

What are the characteristics of a person who influences, one with this kind of *presence?* Consider the people who have influenced you most in life. What characteristics did these people have? Chances are your list will include most of what Legacy Leadership comprises.

We are obliged to offer one note of caution. A person who positively and intentionally influences others is not just someone who makes everyone *feel good.* They will often have to deliver tough talk, or ask tough questions, or make tough decisions that impact others. However, this toughness will be delivered with such humility and committed resolve for the best outcomes for everyone, that people will naturally and consistently be inspired and led by them—to be their best selves. Their presence in the lives of people leaves lasting impact.

What is Legacy Leadership?

Over the many years of our combined experience, we have observed the most common behaviors of successful leaders and identified the Legacy Practices that set outstanding leaders apart from other leaders. When we listened to the deepest issues that were on leaders' minds, they were matters of meaning and legacy. We developed Legacy Leadership as a map for insuring excellence in leadership practices that would enable leaders to not only leave the legacy they intended—but to *live* it today.

We have isolated, defined and made transferable the practices common to leaders who are able to achieve and sustain success—with people, product and revenue. Legacy Leadership is based on five Legacy Practices which are common in all great leaders, whether it be the ancients whose successes leap from the worn pages of history, or the Fortune 500 leaders of today—and will be observed in the leaders of tomorrow. It is a philosophy, a model, and a proven process for bringing out individual best, developing leaders in an organization, establishing organizational leadership culture, and positively impacting the bottom line. It is a balanced approach to people and production. It is simple, yet powerful—it works.

Current leader books and articles cover various aspects and techniques of leadership, yet do not deliver a comprehensive model. Legacy Leadership is a complete framework of practices, behaviors, attitudes and values that addresses every aspect of successful leadership, energizes people and whole organizations, and actively grows tomorrow's leaders, today. *Legacy* Leaders become students of leadership while focusing on building other leaders who build leaders, who build leaders....

We hear stories every day about the lack of strong leadership talent. Legacy Leadership is a broad platform for developing such talented leaders. It includes competencies and practices with immediate applicability to most every possibility and challenge leaders face today.

Many organizations have a set of competencies with which to measure their leader performance; others do not. In either case, Legacy Leadership provides a sound structure in which such competencies can reside. The 5 Legacy Practices form a structural map for a full and complete picture of your leader development program's destination, for you personally and for those you lead. The outcome is fully developed leaders, both current and emerging, and a greatly enhanced leadership potential within the organization. Legacy Leadership makes it easy to embrace a powerful leadership system throughout an organization by providing the guidelines and simple framework for individuals to sustain that culture. It was originally designed for leadership development—at all levels. Every employee is a potential leader, capable of becoming a true Legacy Leader. This system outlines and defines the way the organization does business—in every meeting, every operation, every project, every person at every level.

Legacy Leadership is not a leadership style—it is a life system and a way of *being*, not just *doing*. This system contains the wisdom of the ages structured and packaged for today's—and tomorrow's—leaders. Its truths and practices are timeless, proven keys to sustained significance—and form the foundation for real-time legacy in today's business environment. The model is vital and highly adaptable. Legacy Leadership contains reliable, time-honored principles refined into an intentional, powerful system for success—today and tomorrow—for self

The Five Legacy Practices

Given that leadership can be complex, we have simplified and distinguished five core competency platforms which represent a complete set of observable and measurable behaviors. The behaviors, when used in total, are leverage points for success. We included those practices of leadership that are essential for every leader, regardless of industry or position within the organization. We call these the 5 Legacy Practices. Most major leadership models or approaches will find a fit within this balanced and comprehensive framework. A simple model illustrates this frame-work.

Legacy Leadership®: The Biblical Standard for Christian Leaders. © 2005-2014 COACHWORKS® International. Dallas, TX USA. All Rights Reserved.

Being and Doing

Each of the 5 Legacy Practices has three components: one part *being*, and two parts *doing*. Most leadership models have a list of competencies, skills and actions that contribute to good leadership. *Great* leaders, however, don't just *do*, they *are*. Too often people focus merely on the *doing* of leadership. It is vital to consider both aspects of *being* and *doing*. *Being* a leader involves a certain consciousness, awareness of who the leader is, and how this awareness and core of being drive leadership actions and behavior. As we initially sought to title the 5 Legacy Practices, it became increasingly difficult to apply a simple label to include all the inherent components. We finally settled on titles that actually said what was meant, and were not merely coined terms or jargon.

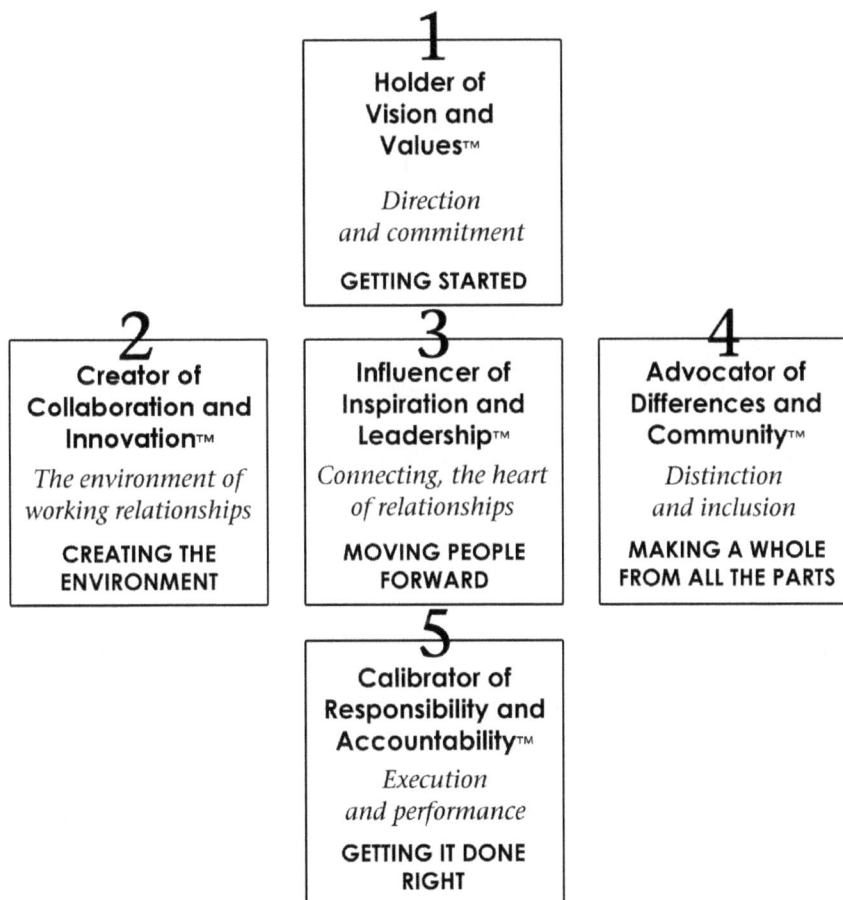

1
Holder of Vision and Values™

Direction and commitment

GETTING STARTED

2
Creator of Collaboration and Innovation™

The environment of working relationships

CREATING THE ENVIRONMENT

3
Influencer of Inspiration and Leadership™

Connecting, the heart of relationships

MOVING PEOPLE FORWARD

4
Advocator of Differences and Community™

Distinction and inclusion

MAKING A WHOLE FROM ALL THE PARTS

5
Calibrator of Responsibility and Accountability™

Execution and performance

GETTING IT DONE RIGHT

When we applied our labels to these Legacy Practices, we took some initial flack about the names. We were told they weren't "trendy" enough, or that they were too wordy. We honestly tried to determine other titles that would be as memorable as these, but we found that nothing else perfectly defines these practices as well as the simple words that define their *being* and *doing*. After ten years of these labels, we're glad we stuck with them. Leaders remember them, and use them to guide their actions. A trendy piece of jargon won't do that.

Here's what we call the 5 Legacy Practices of Legacy Leadership:

One:	Holder of Vision and Values™
Two:	Creator of Collaboration and Innovation™
Three:	Influencer of Inspiration and Leadership™
Four:	Advocator of Differences and Community™
Five:	Calibrator of Responsibility and Accountability™

The first word in each title is the *being* part of that leadership practice. A great leader is first a holder, a creator, an influencer, an advocator and a calibrator. This is the key to understanding this leadership model, and to understanding what really makes leaders great. The greatness resides in *who they are* first, and *what they do* second. What a person does is dictated by who they are. Some people will debate about whether a leader is born or created. We say it is a little of both. It begins with the core of the leader—who he or she is. But even this core nature can be shaped and transformed. Sometimes it is about having what we often call an "attitude adjustment." We've all had those, and often these adjustments can alter who we are in the future. This is the purpose of this model, to shape the leader's core being, and then polish how he or she acts out that being.

Now, like no other time in history, there is a need to develop strong leadership abilities. Using a model with proven success for both the best of times and worst of times, Legacy Leadership embodies a compelling and comprehensive set of competencies and skills. Legacy Leaders lead the way for others to follow to the edge of current development and beyond. We welcome you to Legacy Leadership!

Legacy Leadership: The Biblical Model for Christian Leaders

Legacy Leadership is a practical system that really works with people. It defines the dynamics of human relationships, and collects them into a memorable, flexible platform for successful leadership. These human dynamics, what works in relationship and interaction, are successful BECAUSE they are God's dynamics. It is how He designed us to work together, and the principles of His will and system for human relationships have been available to us since Moses first penned the Torah, the first 5 books of the Bible. Legacy Leadership embodies God's will and ways for us as we lead and interact with others. CoachWorks® has written Legacy Leadership into faith-based concepts, using scriptural references and faith language, for practical application by Christian leaders. Most of the original 50 critical success skills translate directly across with little need for change, but there is one major difference between the secular leader and the Christian leader: **God is boss. It is all about Him, not about you or me.**

Legacy Leadership®: The Biblical Standard for Christian Leaders. © 2005-2014 COACHWORKS® International. Dallas, TX USA. All Rights Reserved.

The 5 Legacy Practices of Legacy Leadership®

*The following is a brief summary of the 5 Legacy Practices of Legacy Leadership®, both for the Business Model and for the Faith Model. All of the concepts, behaviors, competencies, skills, etc. embodied in the Business Model Best Practices are also found in the Faith Model. **But there is one major difference: God is the Boss for the Christian Leader. His ways and will are our first priority. The explanation for the Faith Model makes this distinction.** The 5 Best Practices include 10 Critical Success Skills for each Best Practice. The 10 Critical Success Skills that make up each Best Practice can be found in the Legacy Leadership® for Christian Leaders Competency Inventory and the Model included in this document.

DEFINITIONS			EXPLANATION and DISTINCTION	

1. Holder of Vision and Values™

HOLDER	VISION	VALUES	BUSINESS MODEL	FAITH MODEL*
One who "keeps" in hand those things that are important, by embracing and encouraging their remembrance.	A clear view and understanding of realizable goals, plans and intentions.	Those things considered right, worthwhile and desirable—the basis of guiding principles and standards.	This Best Practice is about direction and commitment. The term "holder" indicates that the leader lives the vision and values while measuring every action against both. The leader then provides consistent focus and direction. The critical success skills include: integration of vision/values into all responsibilities, having a well-defined strategic plan, team translation of vision and values, establishing milestones and benchmarks, modeling the practice, developing the potential of others to pull out the best in them, and effectively communicating and sustaining organizational vision/values.	For the Christian leader, this Best Practice includes, above all else, the holding of God's vision and values, His plans and intentions for individuals and all humankind, and embracing and encouraging their remembrance. The holding of God's vision and values always takes priority over secular vision and values, and never wavers in its primary priority. It includes having clearly identified personal values, "walking the talk" at all times, and intentionally modeling God's principals and values, which are integrated into everything the Christian leader does.

2. Creator of Collaboration and Innovation™

CREATOR	COLLABORATION	INNOVATION	BUSINESS MODEL	FAITH MODEL*
One who causes something to "come into being" through original or inventive means.	The process of working together to achieve common goals instead of personal agenda.	The introduction of something new and different to the process of achieving goals.	This Best Practice is about creating a positive environment for working relationships. The term "creator" indicates the leader's ability to create a learning trusting environment where collaboration and innovation can occur. The critical success skills include abilities to: unleash innovation, listen masterfully, learn from others, be aware of the bigger picture, discern when change needs to occur, and being a masterful facilitator.	The Christian Leader understands that all people are creative, made in God's image, and as such have the ability to make opportunities for collaboration and innovation, where judgment is suspended, trust is encouraged, and disagreement is approached in humility, with a heart to reach others. Real innovation comes only with God's guidance and reliance on the Holy Spirit. The Christian leader always encourages collaboration and innovation, but always tests everything against God's will, word, and ways.

3. Influencer of Inspiration and Leadership™

INFLUENCER	INSPIRATION	LEADERSHIP	BUSINESS MODEL	FAITH MODEL*
One who brings about a desired effect in others, by direct or indirect means.	The process of animating, motivating or encouraging others to reach new levels of achievement.	The process of guiding and directing others to shared success.	This Best Practice is about making connections with individuals—the heart of relationships as well as leadership. The term "influencer" indicates the leader's ability to influence and inspire for positive relationships. The critical success skills include abilities to: influence positively, demonstrate high levels of emotional intelligence, bring out the best in people by developing them fully, focus on others rather than self, make tough decisions with minimal people impact, and be humble while holding resolve to accomplish stated goals.	The Christian leader uses his or her faith, positive attitude and the Holy Spirit's guidance to develop relationships and influence others. Risk taking, tough decisions and accomplishing goals are realized only through the Holy Spirit's guidance, not self reliance. The Christian leader ultimately works for God's glory, not self. This leader understands that God is the ultimate leader and source of true inspiration. The spiritual development of others is a primary concern, and the real work of the Christian leader.

4. Advocator of Differences and Community™

ADVOCATOR	DIFFERENCES	COMMUNITY	BUSINESS MODEL	FAITH MODEL*
One who stands in support of a cause, a practice or a person on its or their behalf.	Those qualities that distinguish people or things from other people or things.	A group of people with shared interest working together to achieve shared success.	This Best Practice is about distinguishing individual strengths and inclusion of differing perspectives. The term "advocator" indicates the leader's ability to support and stand for strengths-based talent. The critical success skills include abilities to: be an advocator of individuals, be a connoisseur of talent, insist on teams with diverse perspectives and abilities, stand for cross-functional development and collaboration, recognize community impact, and promote an inclusive environment united toward a common focus.	The Christian leader's loyalty is to God first, then others. He or she understands spiritual gifts, is able to discern them, and is an advocate for a God-given strengths (gifts) culture. While promoting an inclusive environment united toward common focus, Christian leaders also know they can do so only as long as God's values and vision are not compromised. They encourage collaboration rather than "silo" orientation, in all areas of life. Christian leaders help the community to be like-minded and open to the greater potential of the whole, one family, whether in business or in faith.

5. Calibrator of Responsibility and Accountability™

CALIBRATOR	RESPONSIBILITY	ACCOUNTABILITY	BUSINESS MODEL	FAITH MODEL*
One who "sets the mark" for the quantitative measurement of success/acceptance.	The ability to respond correctly to—and meet—stated expectations.	The obligation to justify conduct, conditions or circumstances.	This Best Practice is about execution and performance measured against vision and values. The term "calibrator" indicates constant vigilance, with possible adjustments, of progress toward accomplishing responsibilities and accountabilities. The critical success skills include abilities to: execute successfully, maintain a "finger on the pulse" for status measurement, require peak performance, provide feedback and coaching, have clearly defined action plans, model a sense of urgency in getting things done and respond to change, be alert to trends, and gain commitment to follow-through.	A Christian leader understands fully that accountability and responsibility come with being a Christian. The Holy Spirit within us acts as the "convincer" (or actually "convicter" according to Scripture) of our need to know something about ourselves—good or bad. He is the beacon pointing out where we might have wavered from God's expectations, and helps us find our way back. But it is only when we are truly connected to Him through prayer and worship that we can see this Light. This Christian leader models the highest levels of responsibility and accountability to everyone around him or her, both in business and in faith, by first seeking God's will every day in their own lives—then living obediently. These leaders rely on God's checks and balances, and require their very best in all they do.

Legacy Leadership®: The Biblical Standard for Christian Leaders. © 2005-2014 COACHWORKS® International. Dallas, TX USA. All Rights Reserved.

The REAL Key to Leadership Success

We hate to say this, but leadership models are a dime a dozen these days. Every week it seems the best seller list is topped by the newest interpretation - or better yet, *discovery* - of the keys to successful leadership. Leadership books take their place on the newstands side-by-side with the paperback version of the latest trend in diet crazes. Everyone claims to have a new secret to leadership success. A new list of competencies, a formula for actions and reactions, a previously unknown secret weapon for the corporate power monger.

Don't misunderstand. There are obviously certain competencies, skills, behaviors and attitudes that enhance and even promote success in leadership. CoachWorks® International, Inc. developed a leadership model based on over 40 combined years of observation and experience with leaders, leadership programs and the use of other models. In working with hundreds of leaders, behavioral indicators for successful leadership practices were identified, and over time, more than 150 leadership skill sets were reduced to the 50 Critical Success Skills that became the platform for the 5 Best Practices of a highly flexible and adaptable leadership model which was branded as Legacy Leadership® – since the premise is that successful leaders develop other successful leaders.

Admittedly, this leadership model was not developed, at least knowingly, on faith foundations. However, shortly after its original creation as a secular business model, Legacy Leadership® was seen as a practical system that really works with people. Why was that? What made this model different than others? After some pondering of this, and humbly realizing we had not discovered the latest secret to leadership success, we saw that the answer was simple. God wrote it first. Legacy Leadership® works because it defines the dynamics of human relationships. These human dynamics, and what works in relationship and interaction, are successful BECAUSE they are God's dynamics. It is how He designed us to work together, and the principles of His will and system for human relationships have been available to us since Moses first penned the Torah, the first 5 books of the Bible. It became quickly apparent that Legacy Leadership® embodies God's will and ways for us as we lead and interact with others. This is true whether you are a leader in a secular organization, in ministry, or in your home.

But even that eye-opening discovery wasn't the real secret behind successful leadership. It isn't the leadership model that guarantees success for a Christian leader, though we'd like to think that Legacy Leadership® works better than most others because it does mirror God's plan for human interaction. Legacy Leadership® works when applied by either secular or believing leaders simply because it captures what works in human relationships. But for the Christian leader there is a major difference right out of the box: God is the boss. It is all about Him, not about you or me.

Legacy Leadership®: The Biblical Standard for Christian Leaders. © 2005-2014 COACHWORKS® International. Dallas, TX USA. All Rights Reserved.

Because of the success of Legacy Leadership®, and the realization that it is in fact based on Godly principles, CoachWorks has adapted the original model into faith-based concepts, using scriptural reference and faith language, so that it might be used in practical application by Christian leaders. But the components of the model itself mean little, if the leader does not understand that the entire premise of this model, and subsequent success for the leader, rests squarely on the foundational truth that everything we do as Christians ("leaders" or not) should be all about Him, not us.

This isn't easy. Human nature wants to "do it my way," and be self-sufficient, self-glorifying and non-accountable. But this is not God's way for us. All the Critical Success Skills of Legacy Leadership are worthless, unless we approach leadership submitted to God, ready to receive His input, then obediently do His will. We always have good intentions (we won't waste time referencing where that leads!), but Christians are also prone to the human temptation to grab the spotlight, to pat ourselves on the back for our excellent skills, intellect and savvy, generally taking the credit from the One who really deserves it, and then trying to function in our own strength. Failure looms around the next corner when this happens. When Christians find themselves in positions of leadership, the temptation to think that God needs us is hard to overcome. After all, it is only because we have superior skills that He put us here, right? Wrong.

Nothing could be farther from the truth. The concept that God needs us is laughable. When Christians become what the world calls "leaders" (though we would argue that ALL Christians are leaders), they should humbly thank God for the opportunity to be used by Him, fall on their knees and fearfully and with great awe humble themselves before Him, recognizing that this position is a gift of service for Him. It is a privilege granted because of God's grace and unfathomable plan, not because of anything we did. In addition to remembering that God is the boss, the Christian leader gratefully acknowledges that God has all the answers, and relies on Him, rather than self and the fallibility of human wisdom and discernment.

In Max Lucado's book titled *"It's Not About Me"* (Integrity Publishers, Nashville, Tennessee, ©2004) he tells of the huge shift in thinking that Copernicus caused when he revealed that the earth was not the center of the universe. He says:

"Could a Copernican shift be in order? Perhaps our place is not at the center of the universe. God does not exist to make a big deal out of us. We exist to make a big deal out of him. It's not about you. It's not about me. It's all about him."

This is the real key to successful leadership. When God places His people in positions of leadership, He does so for a purpose – HIS purpose. It is about Him, not us, and He never fails. Once we realize that it is God's plan, and God's responsibility to fulfill it, and have submitted completely to Him, we can really find success in our leadership roles and life.

Each of the 5 Best Practices of Legacy Leadership® incorporates dual components, in addition to a functional BEING for the leader:

Best Practice 1:   **Holder of Vision and Values™**
Best Practice 2:   **Creator of Collaboration and Innovation™**
Best Practice 3:   **Influencer of Inspiration and Leadership™**
Best Practice 4:   **Advocator of Differences and Community™**
Best Practice 5:   **Calibrator of Responsibility and Accountability™**

In the Faith Version of Legacy Leadership® all 5 of the Best Practices are explored for faith foundations, using examples of Biblical leaders. The goal of leadership is to cause others to follow. The ultimate goal of Christian leadership is for others to follow us to find Jesus. Sometimes that is done by words, but most often it is by example. And Christian leaders develop other leaders by example.

Are you a Christian leader? Have you completely submitted to God, realizing that you are merely the "power tool" in His hands, or have you allowed the deadly attitude of pride in self to creep into your leadership? Lay self down, and take up the mantle of God's headship and power. Become the servant rod in the hands of Almighty God, and let Him part the seas of leadership for you, and ultimately for others, with His power, strength and perfect plan. And, while you're at it, write this in crayon on your bathroom mirror: "It's Not About Me."

Foundational Truth: The Legacy Is His
It's All About Him

You will notice that the logo for Legacy Leadership for Christian Leaders is based on the 5-block design originally used for the 5 Best Practices of Legacy Leadership. For the Christian, however, another cornerstone block is added to the bottom of the 5-block piece. It is not accidental that this graphic now clearly shows a cross—a reminder of just exactly whom we serve, and Who is ultimately our Leader. The entire premise of this model for leadership rests on a foundational truth: everything we do as Christians (followers of Jesus to be literal) should be all about Him, not us. To be truly effective Christian leaders, we must submit completely to His leadership, rely solely on His guidance, and work only as He directs.

As we said before, this is usually not very easy. We humans don't like accountability, and we don't like authority. But all the best leadership advice and models in the world will be absolutely worthless to Christian leaders, unless we approach leadership submitted to God, placing Him in the leader's chair, not us. The following is an excerpt from the booklet *"It's Not About Me: The Keys to Sacrificial Service for God."* This booklet asks 5 basic questions of

Legacy Leadership®: The Biblical Standard for Christian Leaders. © 2005-2014 COACHWORKS® International. Dallas, TX USA. All Rights Reserved.

those who desire to be in God's will, and serve Him the best they can. It also rests these questions and answers squarely on the same foundational truth: It's Not About Me. Christian leadership is not about the Christian leader—it is about the God who made the leader and the opportunity to serve.

1. *Are you right with God?*
2. *Are you right with Others?*
3. *Are you right with Yourself?*
4. *Are you right for this Position?*
5. *Are you under Holy Spirit conviction?*

It's all about God. Not about you. Not about ME.

There is one more question, one that is the key to not only ministry (and leadership), but to your entire relationship with God. That question is: **Are you willing to submit to God?**

- Are you willing to allow Him to have His way with you?
- Are you willing to let Him MAKE you right in these areas?
- Are you willing to make Him not only Savior, but Lord of your life?
- Are you willing to allow Him to be the ultimate leader, the One who gets the glory, not you?

ARE YOU WILLING....?

Savior AND Lord

A Foundational lesson before we begin....

In the New Testament, the word "Savior" is used 24 times to describe Jesus. There is another word, however, used over 700 times in the New Testament to describe Him. That word is "Lord." The New Testament was originally written in Greek, the language of the people at that time. The Greek word for what we have translated as LORD is ***KURIOS***, and the literal translation of that word in English is MASTER. It implies *"he to whom a person or thing belongs, about which he has power of deciding; master, lord, the possessor and disposer of a thing, the owner; one who has control of the person, the master."*

Our Savior's name is **Jesus** *(Yeshua in Hebrew)*. His position is **Christ** (The Messiah, or HaMashiach in Hebrew, Christos in Greek = The Anointed One). His title is **Lord** (Master). It is belief in Jesus that saves us, but God expects more. He expects us to yield completely to Jesus, to make Him LORD, Master of our lives. That means He is number ONE. He is in charge. His will is before our will. That is perhaps the hardest choice we will make in life – it is the most difficult for our sinful, prideful nature. It should be a natural choice following our decision to believe in Him and trust God's promises of salvation through Jesus. But quite often people stop at belief. They still want to maintain "ownership" of their lives, and remain in control.

Some seem to think that by yielding, submitting, to Jesus, that they must give up all the "fun" in their lives. Oh, my. What they are missing. All we give up is heartache, selfishness, arrogance and pride. What we gain cannot be adequately described in words. What we gain, in essence, is freedom from all of those things. In Peter's epistles, he always refers to Jesus as Lord and Savior. Master and Savior. He must be both.

James, the brother of Jesus, writes:

> *"Therefore submit to God. Resist the devil and he will flee from you. Draw near to God and He will draw near to you. Cleanse your hands, you sinners; and purify your hearts, you double-minded. ... Humble yourselves in the sight of the Lord, and He will lift you up."* (James 4:7, 8, 10 NKJV)

The freedom obtained by submitting wholly to God is spoken of by Peter:

> *"Therefore humble yourselves under the mighty hand of God, that He may exalt you in due time, casting all your care upon Him, for He cares for you."*
> (1 Peter 5:6-7 NKJV)

There is great freedom in giving up the need to exalt ourselves, because as we submit to God, HE will exalt us. That is by far the better choice. God wants to carry our burdens, our cares, our needs, our wants, our desires, our everything. He wants to carry US. But He will not do it without our permission. The choice is ours. Either He is in charge, or we are. It cannot be both ways. This is probably the first, most critical lesson for the Christian leader.

Servants

The scriptures also use the word "servant" as in "servant of Jesus." In English, we can't quite get the power of what was intended with this word. A servant, as we understand it, is a person who still has some freedom to come and go, have a life of their own, and make many choices for themselves. The original word in Greek, however, is **DUOLOS**, which means "bondsman" (or woman). The real meaning of this word, as it was used in the Greek culture at that time (even Israel was "Hellenized" when the New Testament was written – under the influence of the Greek culture), will give us a better idea of the impact of what our relationship with God should be.

Slavery was common in Biblical times. A slave could have been taken captive by a conquering people, or could have indentured him or herself to fellow citizens (Jews often had Jewish slaves) to pay a debt. Whatever the reason, the slave was given household duties and was expected to obey the master of the household, for at least the agreed term of their indenture.

Legacy Leadership®: The Biblical Standard for Christian Leaders. © 2005-2014 COACHWORKS® International. Dallas, TX USA. All Rights Reserved.

However, in some cases, a slave would become so fond of a master and the master's household, that he or she would make the free and personal CHOICE to remain with that master for life. They literally then became part of the household, always in service to that master and his family. Again, this was a *free* choice on the part of the slave. They would come to love the master so much that they freely chose to remain indentured for life to that person. The custom at that time, when this happened, was to take the person to the door posts of the house and drive an awl through the lobe of the ear of the slave *(don't grimace, this was just like our ear piercing!)* and then the slave would be given an earring bearing the personal stamp or brand of the master. This was a solemn ceremony and signified the willing choice of the slave to remain a slave forever to this master, and the master's pledge to always care for this person.

Are you getting the picture here? **THIS** is the kind of "servant" we are to be to God. We are, in essence, a bondsman or woman, having fallen so much in love with God that we cannot even think of being away from Him, and therefore freely choose to remain His servant forever. He is the Master. We are the slave – by our own choice. This is the kind of relationship God wants with us. When these slaves requested this permanent servanthood, the master of the house received him or her like family, though they still remained a servant. The master would care for this bondsperson for the rest of his or her life, and in turn the slave would serve this master always, freely and with great joy.

God is a gentleman. He will not impose His will on us, without our permission. So we come back to the question: Are you **willing**...? Is Jesus both Savior **and Lord** to you? Is He Master of your life, or are you?

If you cannot say, honestly and with a humble heart, that Jesus is indeed your Master, that HE is the one in control (not you) **then you should probably reconsider service to Him - of any kind (including leadership!).** God wants your heart, not your meaningless service. And it IS meaningless without your heart. When James says "faith without works is dead" he is clear that faith comes first. Faith is not just belief, it is complete submission to God. The works come as a natural offering to God. Successful service to God flows from a heart freely given over to Him. We have given up the ownership of our lives to Him. It is a choice you will NEVER regret.

Of course none of us can answer a YES to all the questions implied under this 5-point checklist. BUT, the main question is "Are you willing to let God **MAKE** your answers be YES?" Becoming completely right with God, right with others and right with ourselves is a process. It doesn't happen over night. God is compassionate and gently guides us through His Holy Spirit's conviction. This IS a process, and that process is called sanctification. It is one of the Holy Spirit's roles in our lives.

The Sanctification Process

Sanctification is the process of making us holy. The word sanctify comes from the Greek word **HAGIAZO** which literally means "to make holy, to separate from profane things and dedicate to God, to purify, to cleanse, to purify internally by renewing the soul, to set apart and be separate from the world." We no longer do the things the world does, but we do things that please God. We work differently. When we maintain control of our lives, instead of freely making Jesus Master, we continue to live, work and operate just like the world – in darkness and in sin. Sanctification sets us apart from the world – and it is a process, a life-long process.

If you find that you cannot answer the 5-point questions 1, 2, or 3 with a solid yes, then God may need to do some work in your life, with your permission. This does not necessarily mean you cannot be used in service. If you can answer YES! (resoundingly!) to the question of whether or not you are WILLING to let Him do the work in you to make you right, whether or not you are WILLING to be right with Him (make Him Master), then you are definitely ready for service. If, however, you cannot say "yes" to Jesus as Master of your life (and all that implies), then your service is a waste of your time, and God's.

(Note: Excerpted from the booklet, "It's Not About Me: The Keys to Sacrificial Service for God." If you would like more information about this booklet/information, please contact CoachWorks International at info@coachworks.com.)

Christian leadership is Christian living—God's way, not our way. Base your leadership on the foundational truth that all that we do is about Him. It is the only way to insure His blessing of your service.

The Legacy Is His.
It's All About Him.

Legacy Leadership®: The Biblical Standard for Christian Leaders. © 2005-2014 COACHWORKS® International. Dallas, TX USA. All Rights Reserved.

Take a moment to make some personal notes in this space below about the material you have just read about what Legacy really is, about being servants and submitting fully to God in order to be used by Him. Consider also answering honestly the 5 questions presented earlier about "being right."

The Christian's Light: *Sphere of Influence*

"You are the light of the world. A city on a hill cannot be hidden. Neither do people light a lamp and put it under a bowl. Instead they put it on its stand, and it gives light to everyone in the house. In the same way, let your light shine before men, that they may see your good deeds and praise your Father in heaven." (Matthew 5:14-16 NIV)

During His Sermon on the Mount, Jesus explained many things to His followers. He gave them a pattern for life, one that glorified God, not self. Jesus told them that while He walked the earth, He was the Light of the World. But His followers were also lights, and when Jesus returned to His Father, believers became the sole lights of this world—then and now. The Holy Spirit has been deposited in us, so that God's light shines through us. That is a staggering thought. Each Christian is a light, in a dark world where light is rare and sorely needed to walk the path of life.

We need to understand how far-reaching that light can be. Each of us has a wide circle of influence. It is helpful to take a few moments to draw out what that sphere of influence looks like, and how our light, or lack of it, impacts others. This is a vital understanding for all Christians, but most especially to Christian leaders. Like moths to a flame, all eyes are on the leader. All eyes are seeking light.

We are reminded of the wonderful holiday movie "It's a Wonderful Life" where George Bailey (played by Jimmy Stewart) wished he was dead. The angel Clarence asked God's permission to make it so, and showed George what the world would be like without him. It was quite an eye opener to George, and it should make us think about our own influence. We cannot NOT influence. We need to give thought and be intentional about that influence. Are we shining the light of God to those in our sphere of influence, or have we put a bowl over the light? Or, God forbid, are we blending into the darkness around us?

EXERCISE 1: WHO INFLUENCED YOU?

Think of the person who most influenced you in life so far. This person can be either a leader, a family member, a friend, or anyone else. This influence can be either for good, or for bad. We often learn much from the bad influences as well. Then take the time to determine WHY you chose this person. Write your answers below or use another sheet of paper.

WHO HAS INFLUENCED YOU THE MOST? WHY? (what characteristics/behaviors did this person show?)

EXERCISE 2: WHOM DO YOU INFLUENCE?

Next, draw out your own personal and professional spheres of influence. Whose lives do you influence? Where does your light shine? (Include EVERYONE, family, friends, neighborhood, business, church, etc.) And whose lives do the ones YOU influence touch? Draw this out like a huge organizational flow chart, or as a big circle within circles (your choice). Show yourself at the top (after God, of course!) or in the center, and show the names of others you influence in any way, and then those they influence, and on as far as you can go. This exercise is important right here at the beginning of this presentation, so that as you go through the explanations of Legacy Leadership for Christian Leaders, you will begin to understand the importance of your leadership influence, and your God-centered life.

Draw the chart on the opposite page and list all the names you can. When you have completed this, you are ready to move onto the explanations of the Faith Version of the 5 Best Practices. Refer back to this chart from time to time, and expand it. Understand that you are casting light in many places. Keep it bright!

Legacy Leadership®: The Biblical Standard for Christian Leaders. © 2005-2014 COACHWORKS® International. Dallas, TX USA. All Rights Reserved.

My Personal Influence Chart

WHOM DO YOU INFLUENCE?

The Model

Legacy Leadership® is based upon five core competency platforms for successful leadership which we call The 5 Legacy Practices. Most major leadership models or approaches will find a fit within this balanced framework. We have included those practices of leadership that are essential for every leader, regardless of their industry, ministry or level within an organization. These five practice areas form the context of the Legacy Leadership® Model. The final box on which all the others stand is the ultimate vision, values, inspiration and accountability for the Christian leader. God gets the Legacy and the glory.

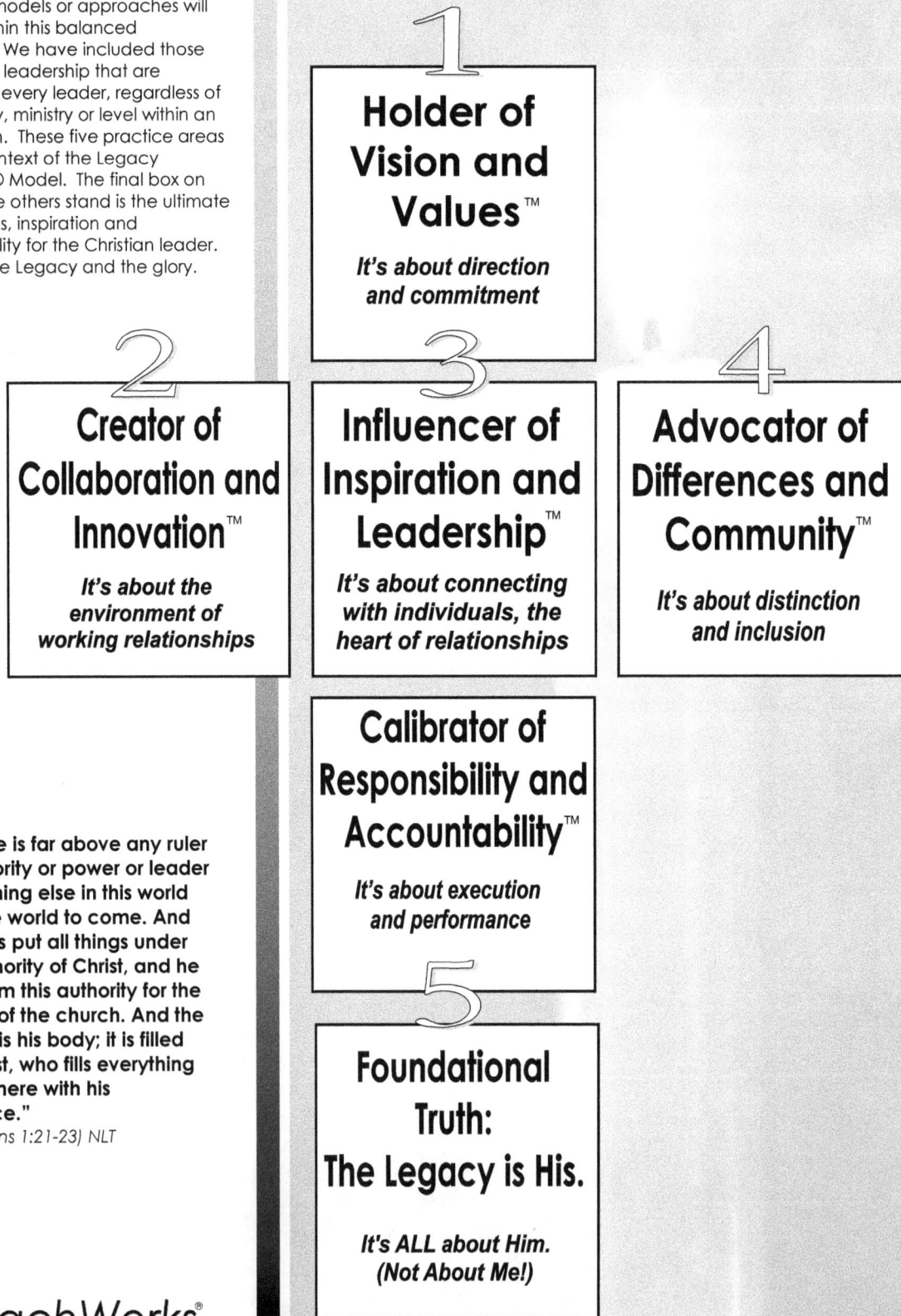

1 Holder of Vision and Values™

It's about direction and commitment

2 Creator of Collaboration and Innovation™

It's about the environment of working relationships

3 Influencer of Inspiration and Leadership™

It's about connecting with individuals, the heart of relationships

4 Advocator of Differences and Community™

It's about distinction and inclusion

Calibrator of Responsibility and Accountability™

It's about execution and performance

5 Foundational Truth: The Legacy is His.

It's ALL about Him. (Not About Me!)

"Now he is far above any ruler or authority or power or leader or anything else in this world or in the world to come. And God has put all things under the authority of Christ, and he gave him this authority for the benefit of the church. And the church is his body; it is filled by Christ, who fills everything everywhere with his presence."
(Ephesians 1:21-23) NLT

CoachWorks®
The LEGACY Leader Company

© 2005-2014. COACHWORKS® International. Dallas, TX USA. All Rights Reserved. Do Not Duplicate. www.CoachWorks.com

Legacy Leadership®: The Biblical Standard for Christian Leaders. © 2005-2014 COACHWORKS® International. Dallas, TX USA. All Rights Reserved.

The 5 Legacy Practices and Critical Success Skills

Legacy Practice	Critical Success Skills
Holder of Vision and Values™ 1	1. Consistently reinforce God's vision and values for His people. 2. Intentionally model God's principles and values in everything with everyone. 3. Integrate God's plan and vision into all activities and responsibilities. 4. Know God's strategic plan (His Word) and align all plans with His. 5. Help others translate and align daily responsibilities with God's purpose. 6. Have measurable milestones congruent with God's vision, and rely on Holy Spirit's leading and correction. 7. Ensure God's values are integrated into all activities. 8. Have clear personal values (God's values); "walk the talk" in everything 9. Place importance on developing faith and potential of others 10. Effectively communicate God's plan and Word to others in order to achieve His vision and values.
Creator of Collaboration and Innovation™ 2	1. With God's guidance, create innovative opportunities for growth aligned with His will. 2. Foster a learning, trusting environment for true collaboration and innovation; slow to judge. 3. Masterfully listen for both what is said and what is not. Listen to God first, then others. 4. Be comfortable not knowing "the answers", learn from individual perspectives, test against God's Word. 5. Draw out differing perspectives, believe that disagreement is a learning opportunity, and approach in humility with a true heart to reach and touch others. 6. Keep in mind the bigger picture while asking timely tough questions in love. 7. Be open to innovation, with God's guidance, test against God's will. 8. Place all plans before God, seek His blessing before action. 9. Rely on the Holy Spirit for guidance and discernment to make changes; help others do the same. 10. Masterfully facilitate conversations where everyone contributes best thinking toward task/goal.
Influencer of Inspiration and Leadership™ 3	1. Be adept at developing and maintaining relationships. 2. Use faith, positive and hopeful attitude, and Holy Spirit's guidance to influence others. 3. Choose to model the positive perspective in all situations. 4. Bring out the best in people. 5. Constantly acknowledge and recognize the attributes and contributions of others. 6. Intentionally seek opportunities to encourage development of others. 7. Lead with a constant focus on showcasing others rather than self. 8. As God leads, have the ability and courage to take risks and inspire others to follow. 9. Be able to make tough decisions, with His guidance, that have minimal negative impact. 10. Lead with fierce resolve, yet humility, to accomplish God's purpose with others. Only God gets the glory.
Advocator of Differences and Community™ 4	1. Be able to take a stand for a person, practice or cause. Loyalty to God first, then others. 2. Constantly raise the visibility of others by encouraging and discipling them. 3. Be an advocate for a God-given strengths-based culture. 4. Be able to discern the strengths and spiritual gifts in others, recognizing, valuing and utilizing the best each has to offer. 5. Appreciate and respect others with diverse approaches and capabilities; believe these differences can make teams stronger. 6. Look for opportunities where unique talent and gifts can be developed. 7. Promote collaboration in other spheres of influence rather than having a "silo" orientation. 8. Consider impact of actions on "greater community." 9. Encourage and maintain dialogue with both internal and external communities. 10. Promote an inclusive environment to unite toward common focus, and God's purpose.
Calibrator of Responsibility and Accountability™ 5	1. Seek to do God's will each day, and rely on the Holy Spirit for "checks and balances." 2. In continuous communication with God to know personal "status" with Him. 3. Be clear about personal responsibilities to God and others, constantly calibrate with Him. 4. Require the best in all you do, and also from others. Support others as able. 5. Listen for God's guidance, and take action when performance does not meet His expectations. Provide Godly feedback for others. 6. Have clearly defined responsibilities (aligned with God's Word) for self and others. 7. Submit personal will to God while planning for the future. Constantly consult Him for benchmarks. 8. No procrastination when God calls. Respond immediately and obediently to course correction. 9. Rely on the Holy Spirit for discernment, guidance, wisdom, foresight. Recalibrate plans as He leads. 10. Gain commitment from everyone with established accountabilities and appropriate consequences and awards.

...and one more:

FOUNDATIONAL TRUTH:
It's Not About me!

(From "It's Not About Me: The Keys to Sacrificial Service to God"
by K Heywood. © 2003. Woodinville, WA USA. Used by permission.)

1. **Are you right with God?**
2. **Are you right with Others?**
3. **Are you right with Yourself?**
4. **Are you right for this Position?**
5. **Are you under Holy Spirit Conviction?**
6. And then...**Are you willing to submit to God?**

© 2005-2014. COACHWORKS® International. Dallas, TX USA.
All Rights Reserved. Do Not Duplicate. www.CoachWorks.com

Legacy Practice 1: *Holder of **Vision** and Values*™

> # Vision
>
> **A HOLDER** "keeps in hand" those things that are of importance, embracing and encouraging their remembrance.
>
> **VISION** is a clear view and understanding of realizable goals, plans and intentions.
>
> *A Christian Holder of Vision "keeps in hand" the realizable goals, plans and intentions of God, embracing and encouraging their remembrance.*

Not that I have already attained, or am already perfected; but I press on, that I may lay hold of that for which Christ Jesus has also laid hold of me. Brethren, I do not count myself to have apprehended; but one thing I do, forgetting those things which are behind and reaching forward to those things which are ahead, I press toward the goal for the prize of the upward call of God in Christ Jesus. (Philippians 3:12-14 NKJV)

Vision can be defined many ways. For the Christian leader, however, vision is ultimately that which God has ordained as our individual and corporate goal – reunion with Him. Our final destination after sojourning on this earth is a heavenly home with our Abba and the Lamb, and all plans in the meantime are still focused on that vital vision. Ideally, our purpose, passion and priorities are housed in God's vision for us. The Word tells us that without a vision the people perish. There is no hope, there is no meaning. Solomon, in his old age and after a life spent away from the God of his youth, realized this as he proclaimed in the opening lines of his treatise in Ecclesiastes "Meaningless, meaningless, it's all meaningless!" Solomon had every thing anyone could ever want, but he was miserable because his vision was not aligned with God's.

From the first to the last words of scripture, God's vision for us is evident. He has a plan, and it never wavers. The Bible is filled with the heartbreak and ruin of people who have not held God's vision. And likewise, it is full of the joys, fulfillment and completion of people who have lived lives aligned with God's purpose. We know that God's plan is most often crosswise with the vision and purpose and passions of this world. It isn't always easy to keep our eyes on Him. But it is the only way to achieve the ultimate vision.

Abraham trusted God's vision so much that he would have given his only son. Moses worked God's vision of His people in the land promised to them. Elijah was holding God's vision when he challenged the priests of Baal to a duel at Mt. Carmel. Jeremiah lamented repeatedly that his proclamation of God's vision was ignored time and time again, resulting in the destruction of Jerusalem. Daniel kept his eyes on God and his purpose while in captivity in Babylon. Ezra and Zerubbabel held firmly to the vision of God as they rebuilt the Temple destroyed by Nebuchadnezzar. Nehemiah reminded the people that their vision was God's vision as he motivated and encouraged them to rebuild the city walls. John the Baptist lived and ultimately died for the vision of God that a Messiah would be sent to deliver the people from this world's captivity to sin. And Jesus' vision never wavered, even to submitting to the horrors of the cross.

Until we are ushered into the mansion under construction in the heavenly city, we have work to do here. God has a vision for all people, and a unique plan for each person. Secular leadership most often does not consider the plan or vision of God. But the Christian leader

24

cannot afford to take his or her eyes from that vision. Wherever we are placed, whatever work we have to do, all of it must align with God's vision and purpose. From the streetsweeper to the corporate CEO, to presidents and kings and prime ministers, the vision begins with God.

ABOUT FORMATTING....

The Example of Jesus

I no longer call you servants, because a servant does not know his master's business. Instead, I have called you friends, for everything that I learned from my Father I have made known to you. (John 15:15 NIV)

Jesus spoke these words in His "commencement address" to His first graduating class of mentored leaders. For three years these graduates observed their Mentor and Master, as He lived the 5 Best Practices. Each Best Practice will present simple illustrations of Jesus' leadership and modeling of these behaviors. These are only examples of the many ways Jesus modeled the ways and plan of God.

Scriptural Truths

Each listing is merely a "sampling" of the countless verses, stories and references found in God's Word. These are not meant to be an exhaustive study of the Bible on the subject at hand. We suggest that you add references to the lists as you encounter the various passages regarding the Best Practices in God's Word.

The Example of Jesus

> *Jesus went through all the towns and villages, teaching in their synagogues, preaching the good news of the kingdom and healing every disease and sickness. When he saw the crowds, he had compassion on them, because they were harassed and helpless, like sheep without a shepherd.*
> (Matthew 9:35-36 NIV)

Throughout the Gospels we read that during Jesus' earthly ministry His whole purpose in being here in human form never wavered. He came to preach the good news, then He died and rose alive again - to <u>make</u> it good news. Wherever He went, whatever He did, Jesus never lost his hold on his ultimate purpose and vision – to bring men back to right fellowship with God. He taught it, demonstrated it through His compassion and healings, mentored it to His disciples... and died for it. Even when the people wished to make Him their King by force, He knew that was not His purpose – at least not yet. He would ultimately return as King, but His vision and mission at that time was as teacher, healer, and Savior. Even when Satan attempted to dissuade Him, He held firm to His vision – a reunion of God with his people. His is now seated at God's right hand, preparing a place for us. He will return to take us home one day.

Scriptural Truths	
Proverbs 29:18	People need a vision.
Hebrews 11:24-26	God's vision motivates to action.
2 Corinthians 4:16-18	God's vision stabilizes, and provides hope.
2 Kings 6:15-17	God's vision provides the reality behind the reality.
Mark 8:31-33	We must be sure our vision matches God's vision.
John 17	God's vision defines our purpose, passion and priorities.
Ephesians 2:11-13	We must remember God's vision at all times.
Philippians 3:12-14	God's vision must be pursued.

Legacy Practice 1: *Holder of Vision and **Values**™*

> # *Values*
>
> **A HOLDER "keeps in hand"** those things that are of importance, embracing and encouraging their remembrance.
>
> **VALUES** are those things considered right, worthwhile and desirable – the basis of guiding principles and standards.
>
> *A Christian Holder of Values "keeps in hand" the right, worthwhile and desirable values of God, embracing and encouraging their remembrance, and utilizing them as guiding principles and standards of behavior.*

"...Abhor what is evil. Cling to what is good."
(Romans 12:9 NKJV)

In the world we live today, values are vague and ambiguous, up for grabs, so to speak. Each person defines values as it suits him or her. There are no more absolute truths. The world has abandoned moral standards for the individual appetite. If it's right for you, then it's right. But God has not abandoned values or absolute truth. He IS the truth, and expects those who follow Him to live righteously – rightly, according to HIS values. What is truth? What is good? The world, perhaps unknowingly, has, throughout its history, shaped its laws, institutions, systems and past moral and value standards on God's Word. How would mankind know what is right, what is true, what is good without that? Yet, somehow, God has placed His code of standards, His values, on the hearts of His creation and reinforced it with a collection of writings by over 40 different people over a span greater than two thousand years. This "book" was inspired by His Holy Spirit, and designed to point - in a beautifully engineered and integrated fashion - to one thing: Jesus Christ. It is all about right living with the right Person – God Himself – and our ultimate future with Him.

In a world that believes it has now evolved beyond the need for a moral standard or values of any kind, God has given us clear directives on what is right, what is wrong, what is truth, and what is lie. He has provided us the definitive Owner's Manual on life. The Christian leader embodies God's values. He or she lives life based on those values, regardless of position or stature. God's values shape the way we do business, the way we relate to others, and the way we pursue His vision for us.

From the giving of the Law on Mt. Sinai, to the proverbs, the bold teachings of the prophets and Jesus' words of right living at His "sermon on the mount," (and everything in between!) God's values are clear, and His disdain for compromise is very evident. He knows we are all too human, though, and Has provided boundless grace and forgiveness for those times of failure. But that gift does not mean we ignore His values. Scripture tells us that we are known by our fruit. That means the world sees something different in us. It does not (should not!) see the same abandonment of values for personal satisfaction. Our fruit is the visible evidence of a life based on God's values. It defines everything we are, and all that we do.

Daniel, at a very young age and having been taken into captivity by a foreign power that destroyed his city and his people, took great risk to live on God's principles and abide by His

Legacy Leadership®: The Biblical Standard for Christian Leaders. © 2005-2014 COACHWORKS® International. Dallas, TX USA. All Rights Reserved.

values. The prophets were repeatedly ignored and even murdered because they proclaimed God's standards. Jesus gave His life freely for God's values. Paul was beheaded for them. All of the disciples, except John, were martyred because they lived and preached God's standards and plan. It's not always easy living and holding God's values – but it's definitely worth the risk.

It is so easy in this world of relativity to compromise God's values in the way we live our lives and lead others. In His letter to the seven churches in the book of Revelation, Jesus pointed out several things that He "had issue" with in their behavior and actions. Even among believers the compromise of values is too evident, usually with a painful price. We must have "fierce resolve" to make God's ways our ways – in every place, with every person.

The Example of Jesus

The Pharisees, who loved money, heard all this and were sneering at Jesus. He said to them, "You are the ones who justify yourselves in the eyes of men, but God knows your hearts. What is highly valued among men is detestable in God's sight.
(Luke 16:14-15 NIV)

The Bible is full of the truth that God's values are not man's values. In His earthly teaching, Jesus affirmed this repeatedly. He taught a different set of values – a set beyond the limitations of this world. Within His circle of followers, He made sure they knew of and practiced those values – He embodied them and held them for all to see. The values never varied or wavered. They are the same yesterday, today, and tomorrow – as is God Himself. These values are based on the high expectations of God for His people, are clearly communicated throughout the Word, and are the guiding principles of our lives. A true Christian is to be known for, and have a reputation for, these values. These values, different from the world's values, give us meaning and purpose, and should be a model and foundation of our authenticity.

Scriptural Truths	
Psalm 15	Godly values motivate right behavior.
Exodus 20, Matthew 5	God has clearly stated His values for us.
Psalm 101:3-8	Integrity is hard work.
1 Peter 3:1-2	Living by God's values is a witness to others.
Romans 12:21	We can overcome evil with good.
Psalm 78:72	All leaders should have integrity.
Psalm 52:7, Isaiah 5:20, Haggai 1:2-3	We often have misplaced values.
Philippians 3:12-14	God's vision must be pursued.
Psalm 18:25	God shows His integrity to those who live with integrity.
Proverbs 20:6	The "Godly" are known by the values they live.
Proverbs 25:9	A bad reputation follows you.

Legacy Practice 2: *Creator of* **Collaboration** *and Innovation™*

Collaboration

A CREATOR is one who causes something to "come into being" through original or inventive means.

COLLABORATION is the process of working together to achieve common goals instead of personal agenda.

A Christian Creator of Collaboration uses original and inventive ways to develop or provide opportunity for people to work together to achieve their common goals instead of individual personal agendas.

Two people can accomplish more than twice as much as one; they get a better return for their labor. If one person falls, the other can reach out and help. But people who are alone when they fall are in real trouble. And on a cold night, two under the same blanket can gain warmth from each other. But how can one be warm alone? A person standing alone can be attacked and defeated, but two can stand back-to-back and conquer. Three are even better, for a triple-braided cord is not easily broken. (Ecclesiastes 4:9-12 NLT)

The Word of God tells us that we are made in the image of God. Many people misunderstand that verse to mean that we "look" like Him. It actually implies that we are made with similar attributes and nature. God is the divine creator, and we can trust that we, too, have been made with creative instincts. This does not immediately suggest that we are all artists and talented musicians, or any other "creative type" that we usually link with the use of this word. It means that we are able to use our God-given creativity to problem solve, develop opportunities for potential and productive partnership, and generally think outside the norms, being constructively creative.

Old King Solomon, though he had lamented a life away from God, learned a number of life lessons. The verses above are classic, and reflect a truth of human dynamics. The last part of this passage, however, indicates a third party, or more than two together. We can interpret this as meaning that three are even better than two, but in God's economy this verse is meant to indicate that two working together WITH God, make a bond and produce a partnership that is extremely difficult to break. The message of this Word is simple: collaboration makes any labor more productive and rewarding. This truth works whether applied in the Christian community, or with secular collaborations. Humans produce more when they work together. The Christian leader who aligns with God, and then partners with others, will see even greater reward.

In this leadership model, and in God's Word, it is the inherent responsibility of the Christian leader to look for, and perhaps even create, the opportunities for such productive collaboration. When we are in God's will, and placing all our plans in His hands, He will guide us into these creative experiences. There are countless references in scripture to the people of God working together, unified in purpose, to accomplish His will.

When the Israelites were delivered from the bondage of slavery in Egypt, God led them into the wilderness to train and teach them to be His people. He instructed them to build a Tabernacle with very specific instructions. Moses relied upon God to help him create opportunities to use the various gifts and talents of the people as they worked together to build this elaborate structure. Nehemiah encouraged the discouraged Jews to bond together and work united in their efforts to rebuild the walls of Jerusalem following their return from the captivity in Babylon. Without the creative and God-given intuitive leadership skills of

Legacy Leadership®: The Biblical Standard for Christian Leaders. © 2005-2014 COACHWORKS® International. Dallas, TX USA. All Rights Reserved.

Nehemiah, this task would have been impossible, as each person and family were more concerned about their own safety and well-being, than that of the community as a whole. Jesus taught and prepared the disciples to go out together to do His ministry work. Throughout the New Testament believers are encouraged to work as a unified whole toward God's plan.

Collaboration doesn't just happen. It requires the creation of original and inventive processes by which two or more people can come together to accomplish common goals – inside or outside of the Christian family. When the believing leader has a task to accomplish, his or her first step is to pray and seek God's creative influence and guidance. If the goal is in God's will, He will provide the opportunity to meet it. He delights in hearing the requests of His people, more in seeing them work together, and even more in showing them His faithfulness and often creative means to answering our prayers and helping us accomplish His will. This principle is true in the home, the neighborhood, the church, the mission field or the workplace.

The Example of Jesus

> *Nearby stood six stone water jars, the kind used by the Jews for ceremonial washing, each holding from twenty to thirty gallons. Jesus said to the servants, "Fill the jars with water"; so they filled them to the brim. Then he told them, "Now draw some out and take it to the master of the banquet."*
> (John 2:6-8 NIV)

At the Wedding Feast in Cana, Jesus could literally have snapped His fingers and wine would have appeared – even in the very glasses held by the guests. He could have merely spoken His healings into being, without relying at times on the fumbling of His disciples-in-training. Instead, He allowed participation in completion of the ultimate goal. Sometimes He worked one-on-one, sometimes with only a few, and sometimes with many. He had the servants fill the jugs with water and dip it out for the host of the wedding. He had the disciples lay their own hands on the sick and heal right along side Jesus. He had the disciples distribute the miraculous bread and fish to the huge assembled crowd. He didn't have to do it that way. Not only was Jesus modeling the behaviors He expected of His disciples, and training them for purposeful ministry, He was creating a collaborative environment where all worked together to achieve the goal. His disciples didn't know it at the time, but they would carry on their Master's work, when His job was completed and He returned home. This was vital training for the huge "team" effort that would soon be their life calling. Jesus was living out an earthly legacy at each of these moments. Creative collaboration would become the means by which God's plan for mankind was advanced.

Scriptural Truths	
Proverbs 15:31-32	Differing perspectives are opportunities for learning.
Acts 17:11	Be open to new ideas, but test everything with God.
James 1:19	Collaboration involves listening more than talking.
Exodus 17:10-13	Creative collaboration can produce amazing results.
Matthew 18:19-20	God is in the midst of believing collaborators.
Romans 14:1-4	A non-judgmental environnent fosters collaboration.
Colossians 3	Peace and genuine love are hallmarks of real collaboration.

Innovation

A CREATOR is one who causes something to "come into being" through original or inventive means.

INNOVATION is the introduction of something new and different to the process of achieving goals.

A Christian Creator of Innovation uses original and inventive ways to develop or provide opportunity for the introduction of something new and different in order to achieve goals, by relying on God's ways, not the world's.

Then the Lord turned to him and said, "Go in this might of yours, and you shall save Israel from the hand of the Midianites. Have I not sent you?"...So he said to Him, "O my Lord, how can I save Israel? Indeed my clan is the weakest in Manasseh, and I am the least in my father's house." And the Lord said to him, "Surely I will be with you, and you shall defeat the Midianites as one man... Then all the Midianites and Amalekites, the people of the East, gathered together; and they crossed over and encamped in the Valley of Jezreel....And the Lord said to Gideon, "The people who are with you are too many for Me to give the Midianites into their hands, <u>lest Israel claim glory for itself against Me</u>, saying, 'My own hand has saved me.' ..."Now therefore, proclaim in the hearing of the people, saying, 'Whoever is fearful and afraid, let him turn and depart at once from Mount Gilead.' " And twenty-two thousand of the people returned, and ten thousand remained....But the Lord said to Gideon, "The people are still too many...Then the Lord said to Gideon, "By the three hundred men ... I will save you, and deliver the Midianites into your hand. Let all the other people go.... And he sent away all the rest of Israel... and retained those three hundred men. Now the camp of Midian was below him in the valley....It happened on the same night that the Lord said to him, "Arise, go down against the camp, for I have delivered it into your hand." ...Now the Midianites and Amalekites, all the people of the East, were lying in the valley as numerous as locusts; and their camels were without number, as the sand by the seashore in multitude. ... He (Gideon) returned to the camp of Israel, and said, "Arise, for the Lord has delivered the camp of Midian into your hand." Then he divided the three hundred men into three companies, and he put a trumpet into every man's hand, with empty pitchers, and torches inside the pitchers. And he said to them, "Look at me and do likewise; watch, and when I come to the edge of the camp you shall do as I do: "When I blow the trumpet, I and all who are with me, then you also blow the trumpets on every side of the whole camp, and say, 'The sword of the Lord and of Gideon!' " ...So Gideon and the hundred men who were with him came to the outpost of the camp at the beginning of the middle watch, just as they had posted the watch; and they blew the trumpets and broke the pitchers that were in their hands. Then the three companies blew the trumpets and broke the pitchers—they held the torches in their left hands and the trumpets in their right hands for blowing—and they cried, "The sword of the Lord and of Gideon!" And every man stood in his place all around the camp; and the whole army ran and cried out and fled. When the three hundred blew the trumpets, the Lord set every man's sword against his companion throughout the whole camp; and the army fled ... (excerpts from Judges 6 and 7 NKJV)

(This is a condensed passage of scripture that tells the story of a very innovative battle. Gideon and the Israelites were up against hundreds of thousands of their enemy. They were "like locusts" – innumerable. But God defeated the Midianites in a very innovative manner – using only 300 men. Gideon was afraid, but he trusted God and led his men into the most unusual battle of their lifetimes. An impossible goal was reached.)

Solomon said there was nothing new under the sun. But this was a broken and bitter old man who found no fulfillment in the ways of the world. He was not relying upon the Great Innovator. In some ways, Solomon was right. Everything we call "new" today is really nothing more than repackaging, editing, or fancy jargon. Real innovation does not come from man, but from the One who invented innovation. We might have some seemingly "good ideas" and achieve some level of innovative thinking the world will celebrate as new and exciting, but to create something truly new requires divine intervention and inspiration. God loves to stun us with His innovative answers to dilemmas. This is especially true if we are seeking to accomplish goals that He has placed before us. But God is also more than happy to help the business believer who waits upon Him to achieve goals that are part of the Christian's work-related pursuits through His innovative means. When we must reach goals or achieve results in some area, it often becomes an exciting and fun adventure for the Christian to place the need in God's hands and step aside to watch Him work.

Because we do embody many of the qualities of God, having been made in His image, we have the ability to innovate – to a point. This ability is magnified and multiplied when it is placed in God's hands, and He is given our permission to act and to lead. Then it becomes a matter of following His lead, into new territory, using new methods and processes. We are the vessels and tools, but the real innovation and the real power are His. Innovation is often just the ability to remain open to thinking in new ways for us, or for our organization. It is remembering that while we may be limited in our understanding, or our concepts of how things should or do work, God is not.

When the Israelites finally came to the end of their 40-year wilderness experience, they camped on the plains of Moab, waiting for God to show them what to do next. Ahead of them lay the Promised Land, but before they could think about residing there, they had to deal with the people who already claimed that area as home. As they stared ahead at the great bustling walled city of Jericho, they couldn't begin to think of what to do. Joshua gathered his brightest military minds to plan. But all their innovative planning could never have produced a strategy or result as great as God's. Joshua sought God's guidance, and God gave him a plan that seemed outrageous, completely out of the norm. Joshua's commanders must have scratched their heads at that one. But, confident in God's abilities and not their own, the people crossed the Jordan river, approached Jericho and followed God's precise instructions. Without lifting a spear, the people watched the mighty walls of Jericho come crashing down. Many of them may have thought to themselves, "Well, that was certainly innovative!" God loves to work in mysterious and amazing ways – and use us in the process.

Perhaps the greatest way for us to be innovative is to never put God under restraint or limit His work in our lives, our businesses, our families, and to always expect Him to work innovatively through us. Our ability to creatively innovate is God-given, and God-inspired. We must have an expectant attitude about God's work, and a sure confidence that there is no goal He cannot attain, no peak He cannot scale, no answer He cannot provide and that if we place the goals, needs and desires in His hands we will observe innovation that is beyond this world. Often He even allows us to help!

Legacy Leadership provides some functional competencies and skills to aid the innovative process, but the greatest competency for innovation is the practiced placing of goals into God's hands.

The Example of Jesus

> *Having said this, he spit on the ground, made some mud with the saliva, and put it on the man's eyes. "Go," he told him, "wash in the Pool of Siloam" (this word means Sent). So the man went and washed, and came home seeing.* (John 9:6-7 NIV)

Jesus didn't do things quite like anyone else. He was a true innovator. When He spoke to the crowds, they marveled at His new style of teaching. When He told them to love their enemies, they were astounded! When He made mud from spit and dirt, people scratched their heads. But the results speak for themselves - a legacy of people who learned to imitate their leader by loving their mortal enemies, and in doing so, confounding them and changing them. Jesus used the mud to make a blind man see. Beyond the spiritual implications of His miracles and His teachings, Jesus created a model of thinking past the obvious, of doing remarkable things with what was at hand, and of embracing opportunities with creative solutions.

(Scripture Truths next page...)

(Continued...)

Scriptural Truths	
Job 37:5, Isaiah 45:15, Ecclesiastes 11:5, Romans 11:33	God works in ways beyond our understanding.
Proverbs 3:6	God will direct us if we ask Him.
Exodus 17:1	Disagreement is an opportunity for great learning.
Revelation 21:5	Only God can make old things new.
Luke 5:17-20	God gives mankind the ability to innovate to accomplish His purpose.
1 Corinthians 2:16	We have the mind of the Great Innovator (Christ!)
1 Kings 3:16-20	Godly wisdom is the beginning of innovation.
Luke 1:37	What seems impossible is possible for God.
1 Samuel 17	Confidence in God, not self, paves the way for true innovation.
Judges 7:2	God alone gets the glory!

Legacy Practice 3: *Influencer of* **Inspiration** *and Leadership*™

Inspiration

An **INFLUENCER** is one who brings about a desired effect in others, by direct or indirect means.

INSPIRATION is the process of animating, motivating or encouraging others to reach new levels of achievement.

A Christian Influencer of Inspiration brings about a desired effect in others by animating, motivating or encouraging them to reach new levels of achievement. This Christian Influencer is first inspired by the Author of Inspiration – the Holy Spirit.

But when the Spirit of truth comes, he will lead you into all truth. He will not speak his own words, but he will speak only what he hears, and he will tell you what is to come. The Spirit of truth will bring glory to me, because he will take what I have to say and tell it to you. All that the Father has is mine. That is why I said that the Spirit will take what I have to say and tell it to you. (John 16:13-15 NCV)

So encourage each other and build each other up, just as you are already doing.
(1 Thessalonians 5:11 NLT)

There doesn't seem to be much truly "inspiring" about the world we live in today. The daily newspaper and the evening news most often serve to send us into a state of depression, or at the very least, apathy. While that is the case for most of the unbelieving world, it is certainly not, and should not, be the case for Christians. Inspiration can be defined as the process of instilling hope and reason for being and doing. We've already seen that without a vision, people perish. The same is true for hope. Without hope, people die inside. They no longer have reason to perform, to achieve, to succeed, or even to live sometimes. Believers have a hope that sustains and keeps us alive. We know there is more than what this world offers.

In a passage in 2 Timothy 3:16, Paul tells us that the Word is "inspired" by God. This is the only place in the New Testament this word is used. In the original Greek, it is *theopneustos*, which is literally "God-breathed." True inspiration is something or someone that has had the very breath of God fill it to give it life. It is appropriate that this word is used here to describe the scriptures. It is emphatic, and God's people need to know that His Word is indeed the inspired, infallible guide for all men, and that it is completely trustworthy, as given by God. The primary purpose of His Word is to bring all people into a personal relationship with Him as Savior. But everything taught in the Bible, on any subject, is vital for first the believer to live a complete Christian life, and secondly, for passing on the inspiration to others.

God guided the pens of the scripture writers, just as He guides the thoughts, words and actions of His people today. And, just as we are able to have a form of creativity since we are made in the image of God Almighty the Supreme Creator, so are we able to provide a form of inspiration for others, as God is the source of true inspiration. He is able to guide us as we inspire others. If we believe that what is contained in the Bible is true, we should faithfully seek to live according to its truths, instructions and guidance in all our relationships. And one of the most prominent themes in both testaments is first love for God, and then love for our neighbors. If we do not love our neighbors, or show them this love, our defense of scripture, and our inspiration, will indeed become the "resounding gong or clanging cymbal" (in other words, just a bunch of noise!) as Paul cited in 1 Corinthians 13:1 (NIV). There is no inspiration in that.

This kind of influencing of inspiration is perhaps the first and foremost for the believer. It is to inspire others to know God. We do that best by modeling God's principles, and making sure our lives reflect Him. In the original business model, influencing of inspiration was meant to provide encouragement and motivation so that others would "catch the vision" or be animated to reach the levels of achievement desired. Believers are able to inspire others only when they are first inspired themselves. And our best and ultimate source of inspiration is the Holy Spirit that resides in us. We first place all needs in His hands, then wait for the call to action, and the words to speak. This inspiration can be for specific people and specific needs, or it can be a life-long ability to model an inspiring life to others. Inspiration does not necessarily mean the motivation to climb the highest peaks and scale huge obstacles. It can be the quiet, day-to-day peace and joy that a believer's life should model, which inevitably draws the unbeliever to the real Source of such peace, the Fountainhead of Living Waters for a thirsty world.

In our daily professional or personal lives and relationships, there are certain skills, competencies and behaviors that we can learn to assist us in inspiring others, either to be or do certain things. It is the same for this Best Practice, and those competencies are listed under the Critical Success Skills in this Best Practice. However, for the believer, the ultimate form of inspiration we provide others is in the consistent and seamless life that models God's ways and character. **We cannot NOT influence**. Everything we do influences others. It makes sense, then, that we make a conscious choice to influence the inspiration of others by drawing our inspiration from the One who is the Divine Inspirer, and asking for His inspiration to flow through us to others. God is counting on that.

The Example of Jesus

These twelve Jesus sent out with the following instructions: ... As you go, preach this message: 'The kingdom of heaven is near.' Heal the sick, raise the dead, cleanse those who have leprosy, drive out demons. Freely you have received, freely give.
(Matthew 10:5, 7-8 NIV)

Jesus set the bar high. This ragged band of disciples was to do more than just preach. They were inspired to do just as Jesus did – heal the sick, raise the dead, and chase away demons. Most likely more than once during their three-year hands-on training their eyes bulged and throats constricted at this thought. Jesus influenced their thinking by stating His expectations. They knew Him well enough that He would never expect something that could not be attained. He had already shown them what had to be done, and how to do it; He now encouraged them to go out there and "just do it!" They were further influenced by the inspiration of the Holy Spirit, the Spirit of Jesus Himself, prompting them, guiding them, and encouraging them to "be all that they could be." This encouragement was not merely for the satisfaction of personal excellence, but for the corporate mission of bringing all to a saving knowledge of God and His Son. Jesus was passionate about His work, wholly dedicated to that purpose. The disciples were inspired to be and do the same.

Scriptural Truths	
Ezekiel 13:3	We must be careful not to follow our "own" inspiration.
Luke 12:11-12	God will give us what we need to say, if we are listening to Him.
John 11:51	God inspires man to say and do what is in His will, even unbelievers on occasion.
Psalm 138:3	God provides the strength and encouragement (inspiration) we need.
2 Corinthians 13:11	God expects us to encourage and inspire others.
Titus 1:9	God's workers MUST have the ability to encourage others.
Psalm 3:3	God is the only source of real hope.
James 1:27	We are to keep ourselves free of worldly influences, so as to not wrongly influence others.
Proverbs 11:10	The good influence of believers can cause others to prosper.
Colossians 3:14	Love is what holds people together, and is the greatest influencer.

NOTES

(Some space for your personal thoughts about what you have read so far, and how you might consider applying to your own life and leadership, or for your clients, etc.)

Legacy Practice 3: *Influencer of Inspiration and* **Leadership**™

Leadership

An INFLUENCER is one who brings about a desired effect in others, by direct or indirect means.

LEADERSHIP is the process of guiding and directing others to shared success.

A Christian Influencer of Leadership shapes and influences the leadership potential of others by guiding and directing them to shared success. The ultimate leadership for the Believer is guiding others to the feet of Jesus, and thereby teaching them to do the same.

This is a true saying, and everyone should believe it: Christ Jesus came into the world to save sinners—and I was the worst of them all. But that is why God had mercy on me, so that Christ Jesus could use me as a prime example of his great patience with even the worst sinners. Then others will realize that they, too, can believe in him and receive eternal life. (1 Timothy 1:15-16 NLT)

The goal of leadership is to cause others to follow. The ultimate goal of Christian leadership is for others to follow us to find Jesus. Sometimes that is done by words, but most often it is by example. And Christian leaders develop other leaders by example.

Moses was a humble nondescript sheepherder by the time He met up with God in a burning bush. Yes, he had been raised as a prince of Egypt, but that was not his true identity. God had ordained him to be the great deliverer of his people from bondage, but Moses wasn't too sure about that. He argued with God; he reminded God that he couldn't talk very well and He should send someone else. No, God wanted Moses, a man who had already been broken. A man who could listen and obey, even in the strangest of situations. Moses was not a natural born leader, but he was the one God used to lead millions of Israelites out from the slavery and bondage of Egypt. We could list the failings of this man, including needing to have his father-in-law Jethro teach him about delegation, and how to handle the complaints and daily affairs of that many people camped in the wilderness for forty years. But we would be hard pressed to find a better example of great leadership than Moses. Why? Not because of any skills, or natural gifts. Only because Moses placed all that he did before God, and relied on His strength and leading, not his own. The strength of Moses' leadership was his obedience – even when what he was asked to do was seemingly very bizarre, like picking up a hissing snake and having it transformed into his rod of strength, or holding that rod over angry waters and having them part so the throng of frightened Israelites could cross.

In the forty years of leading God's people, Moses had his good days and bad days, like any leader. He even lost his temper, a very natural response when you are leading an entire community of grumbling and rebellious people. It was during one of those days that he did something that kept him from going the whole distance, from entering the Promised Land. He got them to the plains of Moab, but God would not allow him to enter, to cross the Jordan River, because of one moment of disobedience. That must have been heartbreaking to Moses, but somehow I think he knew God was justified, as He always is.

The Bible is loaded with examples of exemplary leadership. Ordinary people doing extraordinary things, becoming great only because of their partnership with God. We can read of people like Abraham, Joseph, Gideon, Deborah (yes, women, too!) Daniel, Jeremiah, Ezra, Nehemiah, and Esther in the Old Testament. All these were used by God to lead and show God's people His ways, and his deliverance. They all faced challenges, and they all

Legacy Leadership®: The Biblical Standard for Christian Leaders. © 2005-2014 COACHWORKS® International. Dallas, TX USA. All Rights Reserved.

succeeded at the tasks given them – some sooner than others. But there is one feature about Moses that makes him the best example for this best practice—about influencing and inspiring OTHERS to also become great leaders. It is about showing them, by personal example, the path to effective leadership. It is about shaping the future leadership potential of a new generation of leaders.

God did not allow Moses to enter the land He had promised His people. Moses delivered his farewell messages to a whole new generation of Israelites born and raised up in the desert during those forty years. Millions of these new generation Jews were camped on the banks of the Jordan, facing the huge and foreboding walled city of Jericho. But Moses would soon be dead. Now what? Who would lead them into the land? God had a plan. He always does. Someone had been paying close attention to Moses and how he had led this ragtag band of Israelites for the past several years. Someone caught the vision, and was greatly influenced by Moses' obedience and reliance on God for his strength. Someone was mentored and discipled by Moses. Someone was ready to become the new leader of this new nation. Someone else would boldly lead the people across the Jordan River to surround the city of Jericho, carefully following God's specific – though quite unusual – instructions. Someone had seen Moses do this time and time again, and paid careful attention.

Joshua came out of Egypt as a young man, and had witnessed and remembered the leadership of Moses in good times and bad. The leadership model of Moses inspired and influenced Joshua for all those years. He knew of Moses' complete trust in God, not his own strength. He knew of Moses' obedience, no matter what. He knew of the victories and the defeats. He watched and grew as a leader under Moses' tutelage. And he was ready when the big show began. Moses did not get to witness the incredible victory over Jericho and the first invasion into the land of Canaan. But it was because of Moses' leadership, and his trust in God first, that shaped and influenced the successful leadership of Joshua – one of Israel's greatest leaders.

If we go down the list of 10 Critical Success Skills for this best practice, Moses lived them all. He had to. But perhaps his greatest contribution as a leader was in the faithful reliance upon God and the model of waiting for divine leadership that allowed him to serve as the mentor for the next leader of God's people. People watch leaders. They carefully record every word, every act, every result. If all they see is a leader leaning on his or her own strength, they won't be very impressed. Yes, there are some good unbelieving leaders out there. But without God, humans do not have the ability to be truly great, and they are much less likely to influence and inspire the leadership potential in others. When the Christian leader places the responsibility of leadership into the hands of God, and truly waits for God's leading, THAT becomes the model for greatness that others can follow. Moses' and Joshua's leadership was not about them; it was all about God, and His perfect plan.

(Continued...)

The Example of Jesus

He also told them this parable: "Can a blind man lead a blind man? Will they not both fall into a pit? A student is not above his teacher, but everyone who is fully trained will be like his teacher."
(Luke 6:39-40 NIV)

The Gospels are filled with the leadership development and training Jesus provided His disciples. As apprentices, they worked with Him daily, were instructed by Him, and observed His model of leadership – one with a very definite purpose in mind: to lead others back to Him. While the methods may have varied, the purpose never did. The focus was clear. It had to be. Soon these apprentice leaders would be charged with what could have been the overwhelming responsibility of leading a lost world to the source of salvation. Without their intensive leadership training, the fledgling Christian faith would have died with their generation. Although each had different gifts and talents, these disciples would ALL have to be leaders, and the only way they would know how to do this was through the careful and patient modeling of the Leader of Leaders. Jesus lived this legacy of leadership for them to see every day, and told them that He was "the book" on leadership. If they lived tomorrow what they saw today, they would indeed become the leaders they were intended to be.

Scriptural Truths	
Isaiah 32:8	A good leader plans to do good. He has a strategy of good.
Acts 5:31	Jesus is the greatest example of leadership, the best from which to learn.
Judges 5:2	When a leader trusts God and models His character, people gladly follow.
Esther	Often great leadership demands great courage.
Romans 12:8 Matthew 28:18-20	"Leadership" is a spiritual gift, and some are gifted in this area, but all Christians are leaders and influencers.
Nehemiah	A great leader remembers God always, in all things.
Exodus 18:13-26	Effective leadership demands delegation, and opportunities to build other leaders.
1 Kings 3:16-28	True leadership wisdom comes only from God.
1 Timothy 3	To be a leader worth following in the Kingdom of God, one's life must model Godly attributes and principles.
Ephesians 5:1-2	Leaders must have lives based on God's example.
Proverbs 6:16-17	Pride is at the top of the list of things God hates.
1 Peter 4:10-11	Gifts are given to be used for God's glory.
Job 16:19, 1 John 2:1	God is our greatest Advocate.

Legacy Practice 4: *Advocator of **Differences** and Community*™

Differences

An ADVOCATOR is one who stands in support of a cause, a practice or a person on its or their behalf.

DIFFERENCES are those qualities that distinguish people or things from other people or things.

A Christian Advocator of Differences stands in support of those qualities that distinguish people or things from other people or things. The Christian Advocator stands first for God, second for others, lastly for self.

A person's body is only one thing, but it has many parts. Though there are many parts to a body, all those parts make only one body. Christ is like that also. Some of us are Jews, and some are Greeks. Some of us are slaves, and some are free. But we were all baptized into one body through one Spirit. And we were all made to share in the one Spirit. The human body has many parts. The foot might say, "Because I am not a hand, I am not part of the body." But saying this would not stop the foot from being a part of the body. The ear might say, "Because I am not an eye, I am not part of the body." But saying this would not stop the ear from being a part of the body. If the whole body were an eye, it would not be able to hear. If the whole body were an ear, it would not be able to smell. If each part of the body were the same part, there would be no body. But truly God put all the parts, each one of them, in the body as he wanted them. So then there are many parts, but only one body. The eye cannot say to the hand, "I don't need you!" And the head cannot say to the foot, "I don't need you!" No! Those parts of the body that seem to be the weaker are really necessary. And the parts of the body we think are less deserving are the parts to which we give the most honor. We give special respect to the parts we want to hide. The more respectable parts of our body need no special care. But God put the body together and gave more honor to the parts that need it so our body would not be divided. God wanted the different parts to care the same for each other. If one part of the body suffers, all the other parts suffer with it. Or if one part of our body is honored, all the other parts share its honor. Together you are the body of Christ, and each one of you is a part of that body. (1 Corinthians 12:12-27 NCV)

While all men have been created equal in the sight of God, they certainly have not been created the same. And whether we are talking the world in general, or the Body of Christ, that is a very good thing. A world where everyone looks, talks and acts the same would surely be a boring place, not to mention hugely unproductive. A quick glance around our world reveals the deliberate delight God has for diversity and differences.

Unfortunately, in our fallen world, man has skewed these differences into separators and distinguishers for judgment. In God's eyes there is only one difference between all of His human family – whether or not they believe Him. Mankind has placed arbitrary value on looks, skills, education, wealth, position, power, body shape, size and color and perceived handicaps – to name just a few. We sadly limit our exposure and our collaboration as a whole people based on these false values – whether or not we wear the Christian label.

Can you imagine what the believing Church could accomplish in this world if there were no dividing lines of thought? If we truly advocated for the differences God has given each person and united together with one purpose and passion? It is a staggering and sobering thought. To accomplish His work in this world, God has equipped all believers with differences that are designed to come together as a whole – one body functioning with all parts. Pride separates us from each other, and from God. The Christian leader must overcome this characteristic of the fallen human condition in order to truly advocate, as the Holy Spirit does, for the differences that make up the whole. Human pride says "pull away and be separate." God says "pull together and be one."

An important word of warning must be given here. There is a movement afoot to promote "diversity and tolerance" everywhere. This sounds great, but, true to worldly form, those words carry a more sinister purpose than they first suggest. Celebration of diversity and tolerance has morphed into the acceptance of anything and everything – often at the compromise of God's standards. Herein lies the challenge for the disciple of Christ. This best practice is not just about diversity, but more about the abilities and gifts, styles, personalities, experiences and backgrounds of people working together, and how we can respect and advocate for those differences in order to be a wholly functioning community. This is good. What is not good, is the wholesale acceptance of anything that compromises the Christian's walk, and God's ways.

The Christian who knows God's Word should be more ready to advocate for differences than the secular world. Scripture is loaded with example after example, exhortation after exhortation, and command after command for us to respect, appreciate and honor each other, and each other's abilities and gifts. Moses relied on the differences in the people he led out of Egypt. Together they built an amazing structure in the desert – the very place where God dwelled among His people in the Holy of Holies. The fledgling Christian Church of the New Testament used their differences to meet the varied needs of ministry. Even then they acted as "connoisseurs of talent." God has deliberately designed individuals with differences so that together we are whole – able to do all the work He has planned for us.

This is not intended to suggest that we should accept or promote substandard behavior, skills, attitudes or other differences. And, it is not meant as a rallying cry for tolerance of things in opposition to God's ways or His purpose for us. The essence of this best practice is to realize that we are each made with uniqueness that enhances the whole, and to put pride away so that we can look more carefully at what God sees – the heart.

It is sometimes easier to dismiss people than to develop them. It is the world's way to judge rather than join others. And our pride promotes this behavior without cause, without justification, without the truth, and without even attempting to discover potential. But these are not God's ways, and they should not be our ways.

The Example of Jesus

> **There are different kinds of service, but the same Lord. There are different kinds of working, but the same God works all of them in all men.** (1 Corinthians 12:5-6 NIV)

The apostle Paul was commissioned by Jesus to provide further instruction for new disciples. He was reminding the Messiah's followers of a basic practice advocated by Jesus – that ALL of His employees were of use, but in different ways and through different gifts – yet all to a singular purpose. One look at the seemingly strange group of men that Jesus called to follow Him tells us this. Peter was a gruff and outspoken, earthy fisherman. John was the beloved, thoughtful and compassionate one. Andrew was quiet but faithful, and a loyal ambassador. Levi was despised as a tax collector. Thomas was fiercely loyal, but a doubter. Nathanael was a cynic, but quick to see the truth. For all of their differences, these men were inspired and influenced

Legacy Leadership®: The Biblical Standard for Christian Leaders. © 2005-2014 COACHWORKS® International. Dallas, TX USA. All Rights Reserved.

Legacy Practice 4: *Advocator of **Differences** and Community*™

to become an efficient, purpose-driven team that effectively passed on the legacy of Christ's message to the rest of the world. Jesus knew ALL of them were required to meet that goal. After He returned to His heavenly home, they went on to discover their own uniqueness and individual contributions to the same purpose.

Scriptural Truths	
Romans 12:6	We all have different spiritual gifts.
1 Corinthians 1:10	We must agree, and be united with one purpose.
1 Corinthians 3:5-9	No one is more important than another; we all do the work God gives us.
1 Corinthians 12:4	All gifts and talents come from God.
Galatians 2:6	Every gift, and every person, is equal in God's eyes.
Philippians 2:3-4	Think of others first, not self.
Proverbs 6:16-17	Pride is at the top of the list of things God hates.
1 Peter 4:10-11	Gifts are given to be used for God's glory.
Job 16:19, 1 John 2:1	God is our greatest Advocate.

Community

An **ADVOCATOR** is one who stands in support of a cause, a practice or a person on its or their behalf.

COMMUNITY is a group of people with shared interest working together to achieve shared success.

A Christian Advocator of Community stands in support of a community with shared interest, and promotes working together to achieve shared success (business, family, Church). For the Christian Advocator of Community the ultimate community is the Body of Christ.

Now, therefore, you are no longer strangers and foreigners, but fellow citizens with the saints and members of the household of God, having been built on the foundation of the apostles and prophets, Jesus Christ Himself being the chief cornerstone, in whom the whole building, being joined together, grows into a holy temple in the Lord, in whom you also are being built together for a dwelling place of God in the Spirit.
(Ephesians 2:19-22 NKJV)

We have already spoken of the importance of advocating for differences. We must champion, cherish and constructively utilize those differences to accomplish the goals of the community. What we often fail to do, however, is to embrace the complete concept of whole community. It is our human tendency to group ourselves with others like us. In every city of the world we find ethnic neighborhoods clustered together, separated from the larger community. In every organization we find groups, departments and functions operating and thinking independently of the whole. In every school we find little separate hives of likeness. You know them; you've probably been part of one of those: the jocks, the nerds, the popular, the unpopular, the trendy dressers and the ones we whispered about in private giggles. Yes, we are all part of the bigger city, organization or school, but we are separated into our own little comfortable cocoons of sameness. We talk about community, but we don't live it, embrace it or encourage it. We haven't yet fully comprehended what community really means.

In the early church, the disciples and members of the new group of Jesus-followers dubbed "Christians," understood and whole-heartedly championed community. They had to. They took stock of gifts and talents, skills and attitudes and wisely apportioned various work to those best qualified. They shared their resources and held nothing back. They communicated details and data consistently. They assembled together with one mind and one purpose. When one among them was blessed, all were blessed. When one mourned all wept. They actually and genuinely cared for each one. They functioned just as Jesus intended – as a community of individuals united into one body with singular purpose. Without this cohesive collaboration, inclusion and community interest, they would have failed at their mission, and quite frankly, most likely the Christian church would not be what it is today. There was, and still is, a voracious, unsleeping evil enemy lurking, just waiting for the opportunity to scatter the sheep, or even kill them, putting an end to the community – and the community vision. The advocating of community is vital to the life of the Christian body of believers.

When God shaped a kingdom from a bunch of slaves delivered from Egyptian bondage, He trained them up to be community-minded. The entire Torah *(the first 5 books of the Bible, the Books of Moses, also called the Pentateuch)* is dedicated to the community living of the just-born nation of Israel. Verse after verse contains instruction for individual behavior as it relates to the whole. Our Ten Commandments, a summary of the vast laws found in these books, are a guide for community living, and Godly priorities within that community. Community is a God-designed entity.

Legacy Leadership®: The Biblical Standard for Christian Leaders. © 2005-2014 COACHWORKS® International. Dallas, TX USA. All Rights Reserved.

This same concept is applicable to whatever community we find ourselves part of, whether it is family, a neighborhood, a local church, a business, or the ultimate community of Christendom. There are communities within communities – necessary for practical life – but we must think beyond our established boundaries to have the heart of God for all mankind. God's concept of community is not limited to separated sameness. His heart bleeds for the entire community of humankind, and He is working to build a community of those who love Him and will spend eternity with Him. It is His ultimate plan, and it must be ours, as well.

We can all most likely draw little circles representing the various communities to which we belong. Some will overlap, some sit separated from others. Within each of those communities we should strive to build the heart and soul of individuals united as one in shared purpose to achieve shared success. We must do our best, with God's gifts and guidance, to help the community be like-minded and open to the greater potential of the whole. As we circulate through our separate life communities, we must also be aware that God draws a big circle around ALL of those – they are all one to Him. One day there will be no boundaries between them, no separators. It will be one family, one organization, one community all built up on one foundation. This is the attitude we need to adopt in the workplace, in the school, in the home, or in whatever community we reside. It is the human tendency to divide into smaller and more separated communities of likenesses. It is God's nature and plan to bring us all back together as one family.

The Example of Jesus

> *"...I tell you, open your eyes and look at the fields! They are ripe for harvest. Even now the reaper draws his wages, even now he harvests the crop for eternal life, so that the sower and the reaper may be glad together. Thus the saying `One sows and another reaps' is true. I sent you to reap what you have not worked for. Others have done the hard work, and you have reaped the benefits of their labor."* (John 4:35-38 NIV)

It takes a community to do God's work. Jesus often corrected his disciples' faulty thinking that they were alone in this work of His. Some went before them; some would come after them. Some reaped, others sowed. Each one had been raised up in that moment, with that gift, for that purpose. But one could not complete the task alone, nor could one receive all the credit. The Jews were biased against unfair tax collectors, yet Matthew went on to write a book aimed specifically at the salvation of the Jews. Peter was sometimes obnoxious and tongue-tied, but he eventually preached a sermon that inspired 3,000 people gathered in Jerusalem for Pentecost to know their Messiah. Different seasons, different gifts, different callings, different work – but ALL directed by the same God, and ALL to the same greater purpose.

(Scriptural Truths next page...)

Scriptural Truths	
Ephesians 4:11-12	As believers, our "community" work is to strengthen the Body of Christ, and bring others to Him.
Exodus 17:1	Even in a community of like workers or believers, there will be tension and disagreement, but this is opportunity for great learning.
2 Chronicles 6:3	The appointed Christian leader is responsible for the well-being of the entire community.
John 21:23	Effective and consistent communication is vital within the whole community.
1 Peter 2:17	We must honor, respect and love the community as a whole and as individuals.
Acts 4:32	Community must be of one mind and purpose.
Leviticus 4:13-21	The entire community is responsible and accountable for its corporate and individual actions.
Deuteronomy 14:27	Community members share resources.
Numbers 3, 4	Groups and individuals within the community have designated duties and responsibilities that are for the good of the whole.
Deuteronomy 26:11	"Outsiders" are to be considered and included (at appropriate times) in community activities.
Acts 15:22	Leaders must seek community consensus for the good of the whole.

Legacy Leadership®: The Biblical Standard for Christian Leaders. © 2005-2014 COACHWORKS® International. Dallas, TX USA. All Rights Reserved.

Responsibility

A CALIBRATOR "sets the mark," determining the quantitative measurement of acceptance.

RESPONSIBILITY is the ability to respond correctly to— and meet—stated expectations.

A Christian Calibrator of Responsibility sets the mark and determines acceptable levels of responsibility to meet stated expectations. For the Christian, the ultimate expectations are God's.

"Then I will appoint responsible shepherds to care for them, and they will never be afraid again. Not a single one of them will be lost or missing," says the LORD. (Jeremiah 23:4 NLT)

Responsibility and accountability are two words that generally send chills up the human spine, and are thus quite often avoided in either discussion or practice. The two words go together and are difficult to separate. Together they imply a chain of command, an authority structure, and an ultimate answering for actions. It is our human nature to immediately rebel at authority and the need to be responsible for our behavior, but God has established an authority structure – and it is for our good. He has given families and other groups guidelines for accomplishing his plan through the respect for authority. Like it or not, we are accountable, and expected to be responsible, regardless of our position or place in life, on earth and in the heavenlies.

Responsibility implies that we have obligations and expectations for our behavior. As the dictionary defines it, being responsible means being accountable. Responsibility is the ABILITY to respond correctly and meet expectations. All humans are given certain responsibilities. We are responsible <u>to</u> God, <u>to</u> our human authorities, and <u>to</u> ourselves. Depending on our place or position, we are responsible <u>for</u> ourselves, and often <u>for</u> others.

Responsibility implies integrity. As we use the word "responsible" it generally means that a person will do all they say they will do, or all that is expected of them. This involves integrity, commitment and often perseverance – commodities rare in today's world. In the Old Testament, God often spoke of the leaders of Israel as the shepherds of His people. But most often those shepherds lacked the integrity to do all that was expected of them, and in fact, did all that was NOT expected of them. They were not concerned about the people. They were concerned about meeting their own lusts and voracious appetites for material things. They sacrificed the good of the people for their own self-centeredness. Responsibility also carries the understanding of the capacity to make moral choices. This is true both for ourselves, and for those who follow us. The verse above is a promise of God, given through the prophet Jeremiah, that one day He would provide RESPONSIBLE shepherds – ones who would feed the people, care for them, provide for their needs, and lead them in straight paths of safekeeping. This promise came just as the people were about to be disciplined for their disobedience, and sent into a 70-year captivity in Babylon. It was largely the fault of those self-involved "shepherds" of Israel that the people went astray. ALL suffered as a result – not just the leaders. This is a sobering example of the responsibility leaders have for and to others. One of the greatest gifts and blessings people can receive is to have a RESPONSIBLE leader, who in turn teaches his or her followers to be responsible as well.

When we lead others, we are responsible for our own behavior, but we are also responsible, ultimately, for the behavior of others. It is the leader's job to be sure expectations are clear, commitment is gained, peak performance is given, and appropriate resources are available **IN ORDER FOR others to be responsible as well.** This also includes feedback, encouragement, discipline, reward and consistent guidance. If we expect others to show responsibility, <u>we</u> must be responsible for providing all they need to do that – including, perhaps most importantly, a good role model for responsibility. Whether in a family, a church, an organization or corporation, God's pattern for the "line of authority" we dislike so much requires two-way responsibility: for self and for others.

The world cannot provide us a good model for such responsibility. It behaves more like the evil shepherds of Israel. We must look to God's Word and to HIS expectations for our model of Godly responsibility. Jesus is our role model. He did ALL that was expected of Him – including allowing Himself to be nailed to a tree to die. It was God's plan, and Jesus executed it perfectly. His last words on the cross were "It is finished." He did it. He said He would, and He did. He was responsible to the Father to do what was expected, and He was responsible for all of us. We serve a God who takes His responsibilities very seriously and never fails to fulfill them. THAT is our role model.

The Example of Jesus

> **Kenaniah the head Levite was in charge of the singing; that was his responsibility because he was skillful at it.**
> (1 Chronicles 15:22 NIV)

It is God's way to link responsibility with the ability to meet it. Kenaniah was a skilled singer, so he was responsible for all singing in the Temple. While many of their skills were in the embryonic stage, Jesus mentored the disciples until those skills blossomed. Then they were given the responsibilities that came with them. Peter was a natural talker – maybe a little overbearing at first, but a mighty preacher in the making. Matthew was a learned man who knew his numbers, but his skill was honed into that of a powerful and convincing writer. Each of the disciples went on to receive individual positions of responsibility, based upon their skills and gifts. They were each the right person for the job given them. The standards and suitable tools of each responsibility were individually calibrated by God.

Scriptural Truths	
Acts 17:30-31	Ignorance does not excuse our responsibility.
John 9:39-41	Our responsibility increases with increasing knowledge, maturity, opportunity.
Matthew 11:20-24	We are responsible for making the most of opportunities.
Genesis 3:12	Ownership of responsibility falls on each individual, and should not be blamed on others.
Galatians 6:5	We are each responsible for our own actions.
Hebrews 13:17	Leaders are responsible for the well-being of those under them.
1 Peter 5:1-4	The responsibility for others that comes with leadership should be from joy and desire to lead, not from love of money.

Legacy Leadership®: The Biblical Standard for Christian Leaders. © 2005-2014 COACHWORKS® International. Dallas, TX USA. All Rights Reserved.

Legacy Practice 5: *Calibrator of Responsibility and **Accountability**™*

Accountability

A CALIBRATOR "sets the mark," determining the quantitative measurement of acceptance.

ACCOUNTABILITY is the obligation to explain or justify conduct, conditions or circumstances.

A Christian Calibrator of Accountability sets the mark for personal and professional accountability of conduct, first to God, then to others.

Toward evening they heard the Lord God walking about in the garden, so they hid themselves among the trees. The Lord God called to Adam, "Where are you?" He replied, "I heard you, so I hid. I was afraid because I was naked." "Who told you that you were naked?" the Lord God asked. "Have you eaten the fruit I commanded you not to eat?" "Yes," Adam admitted, "but it was the woman you gave me who brought me the fruit, and I ate it." Then the Lord God asked the woman, "How could you do such a thing?" "The serpent tricked me," she replied. "That's why I ate it." (Genesis 3:8-13 NLT)

Accountability is one of the most basic of God's directives for human behavior. The pages of the Bible are loaded with examples and models of accountability, or its lack. Accountability is the ability to give account for our behavior, to provide justification and explanation – and for owning the consequences. A business person traveling for his or her company is asked to provide an accounting for expenses incurred. It is a listing of the "why" of such expenses. It is the same for our behavior. It is expected that we will be able to adequately justify our actions, and ultimately accept and understand the circumstances that result.

Accountability is a relatively simple concept, yet from the beginning man has had difficulty with this character indicator. The scripture above is almost laughable, if it weren't so very tragic, as first Adam and then Eve attempt to shift the blame for their behaviors. Adam says it was Eve's fault (and even implicated God in that one!), and Eve dumped the blame on the snake. We are all living with the consequences of that behavior. Humankind is no different today. Most often we are quick to shout "Not my fault!" and point to the next guy in line. Today we live in a "no-fault" society. It's never our fault. It was my overbearing mother, or my abusive father, or my thoughtless teachers, or my lazy spouse, my incompetent teammate, or that guy or gal over there. Not me. I didn't do it, and if I did, it wasn't my fault.

Accountability is the ability to truthfully answer and explain the "why" of our behavior, and understanding that we ARE accountable, to God and to others. But for most of the world, it has evolved into the art of making excuses, shifting fault, and disowning consequences. Frequently we don't even consider the consequences, since most have abandoned the idea that we are accountable at all. But God's Word makes it very clear that all mankind is accountable, and will indeed give account to Him for their actions.

A Christian leader must first understand that accountability comes with being a Christian, and especially a Christian leader. God knows the human heart, and knows how we hate that word, and avoid that responsibility. In His grace and mercy, He designed us with something to help keep us accountable—He has made us vessels to be filled with His Holy Spirit. The world calls this a "conscience." To the unbelieving world, the conscience is a vague misunderstood "something" that most often just burdens us and should be ignored. When that word is used in New Testament scripture it is the Greek word *suneidesis* (soon-i'-day-sis) which literally means the soul's ability to distinguish between what is morally good and bad, prompting to do the former and shun the latter, commending one, condemning the other.

Legacy Practice 5: *Calibrator of Responsibility and **Accountability***™

(Continued...)

All humans are designed with a conscience. We know it better as the Person and the work of the Holy Spirit. If we walk with God, we are aware of His leading, guiding, correcting and constant companionship—at least we should be. Unbelievers, however, lack the knowledge of God that unlocks the real understanding and comprehension of the conscience. Conscience and accountability go hand in hand.

Perhaps one of the greatest and most overlooked tragedies of lack of accountability is the barrier it becomes to forgiveness and growth. We do not seem to understand that we cannot truly receive forgiveness without a repentant heart, and we cannot have a repentant heart without awareness and accountability for our actions. The work of the Holy Spirit in every believer's life is called sanctification. It is the ongoing process that makes us better each day, closer to the image in which we were created. Closer to being the man or woman that God desires. This sanctifying process results in spiritual growth and maturity. Without accountability, that growth is effectively halted, and our spiritual maturity is retarded. If we cannot own our behavior, and the consequences, we cannot grow. Our designed and intended purpose is to fellowship with God, bring Him glory and mirror His attributes. Without accountability, that is impossible and we are not fulfilling our purpose and design.

The ability to be accountable is a neon sign to others clearly indicating a person's integrity and spiritual character and maturity. Personal accountability opens the door to the joys and relief of forgiveness. On occasion it also means accepting and enduring hardships that may come as consequences of our behavior, but accountability ultimately unlocks the key to spiritual growth, closeness to God, and effective ministry and leadership.

The Example of Jesus

> *Jesus told his disciples: "There was a rich man whose manager was accused of wasting his possessions. So he called him in and asked him, `What is this I hear about you? Give an account of your management, because you cannot be manager any longer.'* (Luke 16:1-2 NIV)

> *Nothing in all creation is hidden from God's sight. Everything is uncovered and laid bare before the eyes of him to whom we must give account.* (Hebrews 4:13 NIV)

Jesus told a simple parable that illustrates one of the most powerful truths in scripture – we are all accountable to Him. With responsibility comes accountability. With no accountability, irresponsibility abounds. Jesus knew this was one of our failings, so accountability was instituted as a means to achieve purpose – the immediate purpose of advancing His saving message, and the ultimate purpose of saving the very ones He holds accountable. Expected failings are forgiven, thankfully, but only if coupled with an honest, repentant heart. Christ's system of accountability is carefully calibrated and communicated for clear understanding and successful compliance.

Legacy Leadership®: The Biblical Standard for Christian Leaders. © 2005-2014 COACHWORKS® International. Dallas, TX USA. All Rights Reserved.

Scriptural Truths	
James 4:13-17	Our action plans must be submitted to God first.
2 Timothy 4:2	We must be ready to provide feedback and encouragement to others.
Hebrews 12:10-11	God's discipline is for our good. We must do the same for others.
Romans 14:12	We will each give account to God.
2 Samuel 21:1-14	Accountability can be delayed, but never truly avoided.
Matthew 25:14-30	God will ask us to account for what He has given us, and how we have used it.
1 Corinthians 8	Holding others accountable involves spiritual maturity.
Romans 2:1-14	Accountability must not tilt toward judgment.
Acts 2:37-38	As our ultimate "leader," God speaks directly to our hearts to help us be responsible and accountable to Him.
John 16:7-11	The Holy Spirit uses conviction to help keep us accountable to God. Conviction is a reminder from God's Spirit to ours when we need "course correction."
Proverbs 6:25	We must rely upon God's conviction because human judgment is faulty.
Psalm 73:24	God will guide us and help us make correction.
1 Corinthians 8:1-13	Accountability is a sign of spiritual maturity.

*Legacy Leadership®: **The Biblical Standard for Christian Leaders.*** © 2005-2014 COACHWORKS® International. Dallas, TX USA. All Rights Reserved.

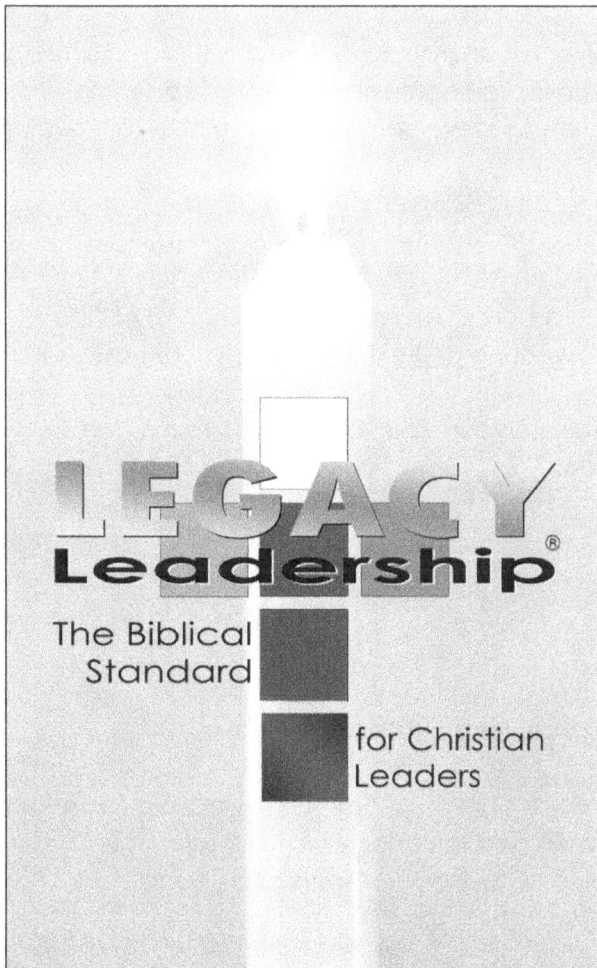

Legacy Leadership: The Biblical Standard for Christian Leaders

Competency Inventory

CoachWorks®
The LEGACY Leader Company

CoachWorks® International
Dallas, Texas USA
www.CoachWorks.com
www.LegacyLeadership.com

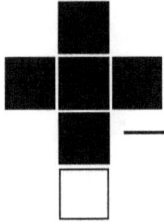

Using the Inventory

This competency inventory is an opportunity for Christian leaders to receive information about their level of competency in each of the five practice contexts of Legacy Leadership. It provides a direction for learning, a guide for leader development and a model for developing Christian leadership fully.

Instructions for Completion

For each Legacy Practice there is a set of ten descriptive statements. YOU ARE ASKED TO PROVIDE A RATING FOR EACH STATEMENT: How often **do I exhibit** this stated behavior/attitude?

Read each statement carefully, and honestly rate yourself on a scale of 1 to 5 as follows:
This statement describes my behavior/attitude...

    1—Not At All
    2—Occasionally
    3—On Average
    4—Frequently
    5—Consistently

Answer all ten questions in each Legacy Practice, for a total of 50 questions.

After you have rated each statement, total each column and place the added score for each of the five columns in the blanks provided. Then add the column score total across from left to right for a total score for each Legacy Practice. Graph your responses on each page. *See the sample page following.*

Complete the Master Scoring Grid.

Next Steps: Legacy Leader® Development Plan

After you have established your baseline as a starting point, you will be able to design a leader development plan including those areas you wish to upgrade your level of performance. See the enclosed templates for a suggested format for your plan. Work with your coach or leader/mentor to carry out the plan and leverage the results. Be sure to invite God to help and lead you as you grow.

Legacy Leadership®: The Biblical Standard for Christian Leaders. © 2005-2014 COACHWORKS® International. Dallas, TX USA. All Rights Reserved.

Rate yourself ON THIS LEGACY PRACTICE, using the following table. Total each column, then add all the column scores for a grand total for this Best Practice. Graph your responses below.

#	Behavior/ Attitude (As it applies to this LP)	Description	My Performance				
			Consistently 5	Frequently 4	On Average 3	Occasionally 2	Not At All 1
1	Reinforce Vision/Values	I consistently reinforce God's visio___ ___lues for His pe___	5	(4)	3	2	1
2	Model Principles	I intentionally model God's principles ___ ___ in e___ ___g I do with all people.	(5)	4	3	2	1
3	Integrate Vision	I have integrated God's p___ ___es into ___ ___tivities and responsibilities.	5	4	(3)	2	1
4	Strategic Plan	I know God's well-defi___ ___ategic ___ (His Word), and align all my plans with His will. His plan i___	5	(4)	3	2	1
5	Team Alignment	I try to help those aroun___ ___ and align their daily responsibilities with God's purpo___ for the___ ___ a positive model, and through discipleship if re___ ___d.	5	(4)	3	2	1
6	Established Measureables	I have establis___ ___ble mile___ ___ and benchmarks congruent with God's vision for ___ ___upon ___ ___oly Spirit's leading and correction if necessary.	5	4	(3)	2	1
7	Values Integration	I seek t___ ___ that ___ ___va___ ___ integrated into how I do business (of any ki___ ___ne___	5	4	(3)	2	1
8	Personal Values	I have ___ ___em ___ ___al values (my values are God's values), and "walk by f___ ___eryt___ ___.	(5)	4	3	2	1
9	Develop Others	___It is very importa___ ___that I develop the faith and potential of others.	5	4	3	(2)	1
10	Communicat___ Sustain Processes	___ ___ffectively communicate God's plan and word to others so ___y ___ ___te to achieve His vision for them.	5	4	(3)	2	1
		COLUMN TOTALS	10	12	12	2	0
		→ GRAND TOTAL		36			

GRAPH___ ___SPONSE___ the table. Complete___ in the appropria___ each of the 10 ___ above. (For exa___ ___you scored "5" on statement #1, color in all five boxes for that number. If you scored "1," color in only the bottom box.)

Rating	LEGACY PRACTICE 1: HOLDER OF VISION AND VALUES™									
5-Consistently										
4-Frequently										
3-On Average										
2-Occasionally										
1-Not at all										
Statement #	1	2	3	4	5	6	7	8	9	10

LL4CL Competency Inventory

Rate yourself ON THIS LEGACY PRACTICE, using the following table. Total each column, then add all the column scores for a grand total for this Best Practice. Graph your responses below.

#	Behavior/ Attitude (As it applies to this LP)	Description	My Performance				
			Consistently 5	Frequently 4	On Average 3	Occasionally 2	Not At All 1
1	Reinforce Vision/Values	I consistently reinforce God's vision and values for His people.	5	4	3	2	1
2	Model Principles	I intentionally model God's principles and values in everything I do with all people.	5	4	3	2	1
3	Integrate Vision	I have integrated God's plan and values into all of my activities and responsibilities.	5	4	3	2	1
4	Strategic Plan	I know God's well-defined strategic plan (His Word), and align all my plans with His will. His plan is my plan.	5	4	3	2	1
5	Team Alignment	I try to help those around me translate and align their daily responsibilities with God's purpose for them, through a positive model, and through discipleship if requested.	5	4	3	2	1
6	Established Measureables	I have established measurable milestones and benchmarks congruent with God's vision for me. I rely daily upon the Holy Spirit's leading and correction if necessary.	5	4	3	2	1
7	Values Integration	I seek to ensure that God's values are integrated into how I do business (of any kind, with any one).	5	4	3	2	1
8	Personal Values	I have clearly identified personal values (my values are God's values), and "walk my talk" in everything I do.	5	4	3	2	1
9	Develop Others	It is very important to me that I develop the faith and potential of others.	5	4	3	2	1
10	Communicate, Sustain Processes	I am able to effectively communicate God's plan and Word to others so they are better able to achieve His vision for them, in their work and personal lives.	5	4	3	2	1
		COLUMN TOTALS					
		➡ GRAND TOTAL					

GRAPH YOUR RESPONSES in the table. Completely color in the appropriate boxes for each of the 10 statements above. (For example, if you scored "5" on statement #1, color in all five boxes for that number. If you scored "1," color in only the bottom box.)

Rating	LEGACY PRACTICE 1: HOLDER OF VISION AND VALUES™									
5-Consistently										
4-Frequently										
3-On Average										
2-Occasionally										
1-Not at all										
Statement #	1	2	3	4	5	6	7	8	9	10

LL4CL
Competency
Inventory

Rate yourself ON THIS LEGACY PRACTICE, using the following table. Total each column, then add all the column scores for a grand total for this Best Practice. Graph your responses below.

#	Behavior/ Attitude (As it applies to this LP)	Description	My Performance				
			Consistently 5	Frequently 4	On Average 3	Occasionally 2	Not At All 1
1	Innovative Possibilities	With God's guidance, I create opportunities for growth (in myself and others) that are aligned with God's Word and will.	5	4	3	2	1
2	Trusting Environment	I foster a learning, trusting environment where true collaboration and innovation are unleashed. I do not rush to judgment.	5	4	3	2	1
3	Masterful Listener	I am a masterful listener for both what is said and what is not said. I listen to God first, then others.	5	4	3	2	1
4	Comfortable Learning from Others	I am comfortable not knowing "the answers" and learning from individual perspectives, but always test to see if those ideas match and support God's Word.	5	4	3	2	1
5	Opportunities in Disagreement	I draw out differing perspectives and believe that disagreement is a learning opportunity. I approach disagreement in humility and with a true heart to reach and touch others who may differ with me.	5	4	3	2	1
6	Timely Questioning	I keep in mind the bigger picture while asking timely, tough questions with love and fairness.	5	4	3	2	1
7	Innovate for Future	I am always open to thinking outside norms and traditions in order to innovate, with God's guidance, for the future, and to be sure such innovation is placed before Him before acted on.	5	4	3	2	1
8	Planning for the Future	I place all my plans and ideas before God first, and seek His direction for how they will work. My ideas are given to God for His foresight.	5	4	3	2	1
9	Discern need (or not) for Change	I know how to rely on the Holy Spirit for guidance and discernment in making changes, and seek to help others do the same.	5	4	3	2	1
10	Facilitate Best Group Thinking	I am a masterful facilitator of conversations such that everyone contributes their best thinking toward the task/issue at hand. I honor the contributions of others.	5	4	3	2	1
		COLUMN TOTALS					
		➡ **GRAND TOTAL**					

GRAPH YOUR RESPONSES in the table. Completely color in the appropriate boxes for each of the 10 statements above. (For example, if you scored "5" on statement #1, color in all five boxes for that number. If you scored "1," color in only the bottom box.)

Rating	LEGACY PRACTICE 1: CREATOR OF COLLABORATION AND INNOVATION™									
5-Consistently										
4-Frequently										
3-On Average										
2-Occasionally										
1-Not at all										
Statement #	1	2	3	4	5	6	7	8	9	10

LL4CL
Competency
Inventory

Rate yourself ON THIS LEGACY PRACTICE, using the following table. Total each column, then add all the column scores for a grand total for this Best Practice. Graph your responses below.

#	Behavior/ Attitude (As it applies to this LP)	Description	My Performance Consistently 5	Frequently 4	On Average 3	Occasionally 2	Not At All 1
1	Develop Relationships	I am very adept at developing and maintaining relationships.	5	4	3	2	1
2	Energy to Influence	I use my faith, positive and hopeful attitude, and Holy Spirit's guidance to influence others.	5	4	3	2	1
3	Model Positive Perspective	I choose to model the positive perspective in all situations.	5	4	3	2	1
4	Evoke Best in Others	I bring out the best in people.	5	4	3	2	1
5	Acknowledge Contributions	I constantly acknowledge and recognize the attributes and contributions of others.	5	4	3	2	1
6	Delegate for Development	I intentionally seek opportunities to encourage the development of others, both personally, (professionally, if applicable) and spiritually.	5	4	3	2	1
7	Showcase Others	I lead with a constant focus on showcasing others rather than myself.	5	4	3	2	1
8	Inspiring Risk Taker	As God leads me (and only then!), I have the ability and courage to take risks and inspire others to follow.	5	4	3	2	1
9	Minimize Negative Impact	I am able to make tough decisions, with His guidance, that have minimal negative impact.	5	4	3	2	1
10	Achievement with Humility, Resolve	I have a fierce resolve, yet humility, to accomplish God's purposes, together with others. Only God gets the glory, not me.	5	4	3	2	1
		COLUMN TOTALS					
		➡ **GRAND TOTAL**					

GRAPH YOUR RESPONSES in the table. Completely color in the appropriate boxes for each of the 10 statements above. (For example, if you scored "5" on statement #1, color in all five boxes for that number. If you scored "1," color in only the bottom box.)

Rating	LEGACY PRACTICE 3: INFLUENCER OF INSPIRATION AND LEADERSHIP™									
5-Consistently										
4-Frequently										
3-On Average										
2-Occasionally										
1-Not at all										
Statement #	1	2	3	4	5	6	7	8	9	10

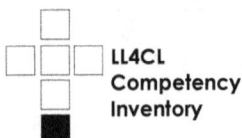

LL4CL Competency Inventory

Legacy Leadership®: The Biblical Standard for Christian Leaders. © 2005-2014 COACHWORKS® International. Dallas, TX USA. All Rights Reserved.

4

Rate yourself ON THIS LEGACY PRACTICE, using the following table. Total each column, then add all the column scores for a grand total for this Best Practice. Graph your responses below.

#	Behavior/ Attitude (As it applies to this LP)	Description	My Performance Consistently 5	Frequently 4	On Average 3	Occasionally 2	Not At All 1
1	Ready Advocate	I am able to take a stand for a person, practice, or cause. My first loyalty is to God, then to others.	5	4	3	2	1
2	Mentor for Visibility	I constantly raise the visibility of individuals by encouraging and discipling (developing) them, as God gives me opportunity.	5	4	3	2	1
3	Strengths-Based Culture	I am an advocate for a God-given strengths-based culture where everyone works from their strengths, and understands their unique gifts.	5	4	3	2	1
4	Recognize gifts and strengths	I am able to discern the strengths and spiritual gifts in others, recognizing, valuing and utilizing the best each person has to offer.	5	4	3	2	1
5	Team Diversity	I appreciate and respect others who have diverse approaches and capabilities, and believe these differences can make teams stronger.	5	4	3	2	1
6	Outside Opportunities	I look for opportunities outside my immediate "circle" where unique talent and gifts can be developed (including business, church, home, and other places of influence).	5	4	3	2	1
7	No "silo" orientation	I promote collaboration among all those around me, including with those in different spheres of influence, rather than maintain a "silo" orientation.	5	4	3	2	1
8	Consider Greater Community	I consider the impact of actions on the "greater community" (of believers, friends, family, business associates and others) beyond my immediate area of influence.	5	4	3	2	1
9	Internal-External Dialogue	I encourage and maintain dialogue and involvement with both internal and external communities (beyond my immediate area of influence).	5	4	3	2	1
10	United Inclusive Environment	I promote an inclusive environment that unites towards a common focus, especially among fellow believers, but also among those of differing faiths and values, as long as I am not compromising God's values and purpose for me.	5	4	3	2	1
		COLUMN TOTALS					
		➡ **GRAND TOTAL**					

GRAPH YOUR RESPONSES in the table. Completely color in the appropriate boxes for each of the 10 statements above. (For example, if you scored "5" on statement #1, color in all five boxes for that number. If you scored "1," color in only the bottom box.)

Rating	LEGACY PRACTICE 4: ADVOCATOR OF DIFFERENCES AND COMMUNITY™									
5-Consistently										
4-Frequently										
3-On Average										
2-Occasionally										
1-Not at all										
Statement #	1	2	3	4	5	6	7	8	9	10

LL4CL Competency Inventory

5

Rate yourself ON THIS LEGACY PRACTICE, using the following table. Total each column, then add all the column scores for a grand total for this Best Practice. Graph your responses below.

#	Behavior/ Attitude (As it applies to this LP)	Description	My Performance				
			Consistently 5	Frequently 4	On Average 3	Occasionally 2	Not At All 1
1	God's Plan with Checks and Balances	I seek to do God's will each day, and rely on His Holy Spirit to use his "checks and balances" with me in order to achieve His goals in me and through me.	5	4	3	2	1
2	Know Milestone Status	I am in continuous communication with God (through prayer and meditation on His Word) to know my personal "status" with Him, and His plan for me.	5	4	3	2	1
3	Clear about Responsibilities	I am clear about my responsibilities to God and others, and I am constantly calibrating with Him and others to be sure we are in alignment with His will.	5	4	3	2	1
4	Require Peak Performance/ Support	I require the best in all I do, and also from others. As I am able, I support others with resources and with prayer and encouragement.	5	4	3	2	1
5	Feedback and Appropriate Action	I listen for God's guidance (His coaching) about my performance and take action when that performance does not meet His expectations. In addition, I offer feedback in a loving and gentle manner to others, and if necessary or required by my position, take action when their performance does not meet God's expectations.	5	4	3	2	1
6	Defined Accountabilities	I have clearly defined accountabilities (God's Word) for myself and for those for whom I am responsible or mentoring.	5	4	3	2	1
7	Action Plan with Provision for Adjustments	My action plan is God's plan for my life, and I have submitted my will to His in this regard. While I also plan for my future, those plans are always submitted to God for His approval. He provides the benchmarks and milestones, as well as provisions for making adjustments along the way. I constantly consult my God for alignment with Him and His will.	5	4	3	2	1
8	Urgency in response/ change	When God calls, I don't procrastinate. I respond obediently and immediately to accomplish His will, and to make changes as He leads.	5	4	3	2	1
9	Holy Spirit discernment, Recalibration	I rely on the Holy Spirit to guide me and to give me discernment, wisdom and foresight as needed. As He leads, I am able to re-calibrate action plans where necessary.	5	4	3	2	1
10	Team Commitment, Appropriate Consequences	I have gained commitment from everyone in my areas of responsibility, and have established accountabilities with appropriate consequences and rewards.	5	4	3	2	1
		COLUMN TOTALS					
		➡ **GRAND TOTAL**					

GRAPH YOUR RESPONSES in the table. Completely color in the appropriate boxes for each of the 10 statements above. (For example, if you scored "5" on statement #1, color in all five boxes for that number. If you scored "1," color in only the bottom box.)

LL4CL Competency

Rating	LEGACY PRACTICE 5: CALIBRATOR OF RESPONSIBILITY AND ACCOUNTABILITY™									
5-Consistently										
4-Frequently										
3-On Average										
2-Occasionally										
1-Not at all										
Statement #	1	2	3	4	5	6	7	8	9	10

Legacy Leadership®: The Biblical Standard for Christian Leaders. © 2005-2014 COACHWORKS® International. Dallas, TX USA. All Rights Reserved.

Master Scoring Grid

Transfer the total scores from each Legacy Practice page.

TOTAL SCORES And LEVELS	Legacy Practice				
	1 Holder of Vision and Values™	2 Creator of Collaboration and Innovation™	3 Influencer of Inspiration and Leadership™	4 Advocator of Differences and Community™	5 Calibrator of Responsibility and Accountability™
Practice Mastery	☆ 46-50	☆ 46-50	☆ 46-50	☆ 46-50	☆ 46-50
Practice Proficiency	☐ 40-45	☐ 40-45	☐ 40-45	☐ 40-45	☐ 40-45
Practice Apprenticeship	○ 25-39	○ 25-39	○ 25-39	○ 25-39	○ 25-39
Practice Knowledge	⬡ 16-24	⬡ 16-24	⬡ 16-24	⬡ 16-24	⬡ 16-24
Practice Awareness	△ 10-15	△ 10-15	△ 10-15	△ 10-15	△ 10-15

LL4CL
Competency
Inventory

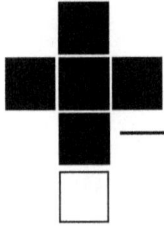

Leadership Development Plan

This is a sample development plan. Other more detailed plans follow. These development plans were originally designed for secular, professional use, but can be easily applied to spiritual development. Use this page to commit in writing your plan for development. Work with your coach (and especially the Holy Coach!) to carry out the plan and leverage the results.

A – KEY PARTICIPANTS
(Name those individuals who will be most involved in helping you track success and holding you accountable.)

Name:

Coach:

Others:

B – BEST PRACTICE DEVELOPMENT AREAS

Competency Areas:
(List the one or two Legacy Practices in which development is a priority.)

Other(s):
(List the skills from the LL4CLCI that you want to work on specifically.)

C - GOALS
(Develop a goal statement that states exactly what you want to accomplish for each of these development areas .)

D – BEHAVIOR CHANGES
(What new behavior will you and others be observing as you are successful in these development areas?)

E - MEASURABLES
(How will you measure these successes?)

F - IMPACT
(What do you see as the impact of making these changes? On self? On others? On your business? On your family?)

Legacy Leadership®: The Biblical Standard for Christian Leaders. © 2005-2014 COACHWORKS® International. Dallas, TX USA. All Rights Reserved.

Development Plan: PART 2

LEGACY PRACTICE	Top 3 Strengths in this Best Practice	Top 3 Challenges in this Best Practice (development opportunities)	Specific skills in this Best Practice I want to develop	My goals for development of this Best Practice
1 Holder of Vision and Values™	1. 2. 3.	1. 2. 3.		
2 Creator of Collaboration and Innovation™	1. 2. 3.	1. 2. 3.		
3 Influencer of Inspiration and Leadership™	1. 2. 3.	1. 2. 3.		
4 Advocator of Differences and Community™	1. 2. 3.	1. 2. 3.		
5 Calibrator of Responsibility and Accountability™	1. 2. 3.	1. 2. 3.		

CIRCLE THE TOP 5 AREAS YOU WISH TO DEVELOP NOW

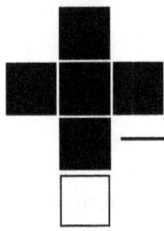

Development Notes

Legacy Leadership®: The Biblical Standard for Christian Leaders. © 2005-2014 COACHWORKS® International. Dallas, TX USA. All Rights Reserved.

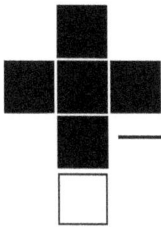

Personal Commitment to Development

I understand that to be an effective Christian leader I must:

- Acknowledge that God is in control, not me
- Desire to give Him the glory
- Want to be used effectively by Him in leadership and other ministry
- Base my leadership on His guidelines and direction
- Work daily with God's help to draw closer to Him, and
- Consistently improve my Godly character and leadership abilities

It is my real desire to do all of the above, and to truly BEING and LIVING as a Christian in leadership and elsewhere. I know that I have human failings, and I am thankful for God's forgiveness which He richly affords to me. I know I need His daily guidance to achieve His purpose for me as a leader, and as a child of God.

Therefore, I hereby recommit myself to my God and my Savior. I will place Him first in all things, and I will wait upon Him for His leading. I will work diligently, with the hand of guidance by His Holy Spirit, to become all that He wants me to be, and to do all that He has prepared for me to do. I submit myself to His leadership.

(On a personal level) I will also:

_____

_____

_____

_____

_____

_____

I promise to do this to the best of my ability, and with His help.

Thank you, Lord, for your faithfulness, loyalty and patience. Mold me and make me into the leader you desire.

Signed   Date

_____   _____

Additional Notes...

Legacy Leadership®: *The Biblical Standard for Christian Leaders.* © 2005-2014 COACHWORKS® International. Dallas, TX USA. All Rights Reserved.

www.ingramcontent.com/pod-product-compliance
Lightning Source LLC
Chambersburg PA
CBHW081157090426

42736CB00017B/3367